Family Worship Hymnal

Hymns for Home and School

Christian Liberty Press

Arlington Heights, Illinois

Most hymns taken from *Songs of Hope*
Compiled by E. O. Excell © 1928
Originally published by Hope Publishing Company

Published by
Christian Liberty Press
502 West Euclid Avenue
Arlington Heights, Illinois 60004
www.christianlibertypress.com

Compiled and edited by Michael J. McHugh
Layout by Edward J. Shewan
Production assistance by Lina King
Copyediting by Diane C. Olson
Cover design by Bob Fine

All Scripture references are from the King James Version of the Holy Bibl

Family Worship Hymnal Standard Edition
ISBN 978-1-932971-19-4
         1-932971-19-X

Family Worship Hymnal Accompanist Edition
ISBN 978-1-930092-81-5
         1-930092-81-4

Printed in the United States of America

Contents

Christian Liberty Anthem

Lord, We Give Thee Thanks

Introduction

It was Martin Luther who stated, "… next to the Word of God, the noble art of music is the greatest treasure in the world."

The gift of music is a wonderful treasure indeed! Countless homes and churches have been blessed over the centuries by songs of praise and worship to Almighty God and by songs that remind us of the value of friendship, love, and freedom. It is through the singing of songs and hymns that God often chooses to unite hearts and kindle deeper sentiments of affection within the souls of His creatures. How much poorer would we be without the blest memory of past days that were spent in the happy exercise of singing?

As the human race enters upon the opening of the twenty-first century, it often appears to be in a headlong pursuit to destroy itself as fast as possible. The love of many has grown cold, as families and communities struggle just to survive in the wake of fractured relationships and increasing violence. Could it be that modern Americans, with all of their sophistication and high-tech gadgets, have lost the ability to relate to each other on a personal level? If the answer to this question is yes, then it is proper to also ask, "What can be done to bring families and communities together again?"

The answer, I believe, lies principally in reviving the old practice of family worship and prayer. History teaches us that the family that prays and sings together, stays together. The first step, then, must be for every soul to acknowledge the Lordship of Christ and to embrace the Gospel. Once this vital move has been made, the next step is quite easy; simply turn off your television and video games and gather your whole family around the piano or guitar to sing.

Although it is sometimes difficult to push aside the clamor of the world and its alluring toys for the simple pleasure of singing with loved ones, your diligence will be greatly rewarded. The song collection that follows will help you to get started in the noble task of family worship, and it will also be a genuine source of good old-fashioned fun.

The hymnal that follows is not arranged in any special order. As a result, you may choose to utilize the hymns in any order that appeals to your family. An extensive section containing some of the Psalms and several responsive readings is printed at the back of this book to provide individuals with the opportunity to incorporate the reading of

Scripture into the routine of family worship. Families may wish to commit one of the Scripture selections to memory each week.

May your love for God, music, and your fellowman grow as you utilize the *Family Worship Hymnal.*

Michael J. McHugh

Benefits of Hymn Singing

1. Hymns help us in our worship of God, both on a personal and corporate level. (Matthew 26:26-30 and Psalm 100:1-4)

2. Singing spiritual songs from the heart helps the people of God to be strengthened by the Holy Spirit in the inner man. (Ephesians 5:17-21)

3. God uses hymns to transmit courage and spiritual strength to His people so they can withstand trials or temptations. Paul and Silas sang while in prison. (Acts 16:16-32)

4. The Lord inhabits the praises of His people and has ordained that His children make a joyful noise. (Psalm 66:1-4 and Psalm 22:1-4)

5. Singing praises to God promotes unity as God's people lift up their voices as one sound unto the Lord. (2 Chronicles 5:11-14)

6. Singing hymns is excellent preparation for the life to come, for the saints of God will be praising the Lord for all eternity. (Revelation 15:1-4)

7. Sacred music has the God-given capacity to reach the hearts of people and affect their emotions and spirits. (1 Samuel 16:13-23 and James 5:13)

The Importance of Family Worship

"Behold, how good and how pleasant it is for brethren to dwell together in unity! It is like the precious ointment upon the head, that ran down upon the beard, even Aaron's beard, that went down to the skirts of his garments. As the dew of Hermon, and as the dew that descended upon the mountains of Zion: for there the Lord commanded the blessing, even life for evermore" (Psalm 133).

Family unity and peace is a blessing that cannot be overrated. This selection is designed to show that it is directly promoted by family worship.

The deliberate and consistent assembly of a whole household for the purpose of praise and worship of God, provides more than simply the means of bringing the several members together. There are striking differences among families in regard to the simple quality of cohesion. While some are a bare collection of so many particles, without mutual attraction, others are consolidated into a unity of love. Many scattering influences are at work. Some of these may be attributed to a lack of system and regularity; some to late hours; some to peculiarities of business; some to fashion; and some to the influences of vice. From one or several of these influences we see domestic harmony impaired. Parents and children meet only at their meals, and not even at all of these. The tardy inmates of the house descend in the morning at any hour, and at long intervals, and the evening is often despoiled of the charm of home. In such circumstances, the links of family affection are inevitably tarnished, if not worn away. In proportion as the subjects of mutual obligation live apart, they will cease to care for one another. No customs of society are laudable or safe which tend, in any considerable degree, to separate parents from children, and brothers from sisters. It is good to bring together the coals on the domestic hearth. Hence we have always looked with unqualified satisfaction on the New England custom of gathering all the members of a family, however remote, under the paternal roof on the day of annual thanksgiving. There is a sacred virtue in even beholding the face of an aged father and a gentle beloved mother. On this very principle, the president of a prestigious college, justly celebrated for his influence on young men, was accustomed, when he saw the first sign of rebellion in a student, to call him to his study, and kindly propose to him a simple visit to his parents. We do not wonder that the effect was often magical.

Family worship assembles the household twice every day, and that in a deliberate and solemn manner. No individual is missing. This is the law of the house from childhood to old age. The observance is as stated as the daily meals. Other employments and engagements are made to bow to this, until it becomes the irreversible rule of the little commonwealth. Such assemblies provide opportunities for each family member to look upon one another's faces and exchange kind words and gentle wishes. Such influences, which may seem rather trivial, rise to inestimable magnitude when multiplied through all the days of long years, that is, over the entire progress of family life. By those who have enjoyed them, they can never be forgotten. Such households stand in open contrast to those where parents and children, in haste and disorder, and with many interruptions, snatch their daily bread, without so much as a word of discussion, thanks, or prayer.

Some good results, in respect of harmony, ensue, when a household purposely assembles for the common pursuit of any lawful object whatever. Union, and the sentiment of union, are promoted by joint participation, and the effect is appreciable where the gathering is frequent. Though it were only for exercise or recreation, for the practice of music, for an evening perusal of useful books, still there would be a contribution to mutual acquaintance and regard. But how much stronger is the operation of this principle when the avowed object of the meeting is to seek the face of God, and to invoke His blessing!

There is no way in which we can more surely increase mutual love than by praying for one another. If you would retain warmth of affection for an absent friend, pray for him. If you would live in the regards of another, beseech him to pray for you. If you would conquer enmity in your own soul towards one who has wronged you, pray for him. Dissension or coldness cannot abide between those who bear each other to God's throne in supplication. It is what we meet to do at family worship. Often has the tenderness of a half-dying attachment been renewed and made young again, when the parties have found themselves kneeling before the mercy seat. Every thing connected with such utterance of mutual good-will in the domestic worship tends to foster it, and thus the daily prayers are as the dews of Hermon.

The devotions of the household are commonly conducted by the parent, and parental affection often needs such an outlet. The son or the daughter might otherwise remain ignorant of the anxieties of the father. There are yearnings which the parent cannot express to man, not even to a child, but which must be poured forth to God, and which have their appropriate channel in the daily prayer. The hearing of such petitions, gushing warm from the heart, and the participation of such emotions, cannot but sometimes reach the stubborn childish mind, and tend to a strong and reigning affection. Both parent and child, if they are ever touched with genuine love, must experience it when they come together before their God and Savior.

That revelation of divine truth that is perpetually expressed or implied in family worship, in Scripture, in psalms, and in prayers, enjoins this very peace and affection. The New Testament presents it in every page. The Word of God and prayer are, from day to day, bringing the duty constantly before the conscience. The household that is subjected to this forming influence, may be expected, more than others, to be a household of peace.

Some notice must here be taken of a painful but common case. Human depravity sometimes breaks forth in friction and strife, among members of the same brotherhood, and, alas, even within the sacred limits of a Christian house. Harsh tempers, sour looks, moody silence, grudges, bitter words, and alienations, mar the beauty of the family circle. Therefore, we find slights, angry rebukes, suspicions, and recriminations entrenched in the home. Happy, indeed, is that household over which these black clouds do not sometimes hover. But what means shall we seek to dispel them? The family altar! Only an extraordinarily obstinate sinner will be able to let the sun go down upon his wrath when he is obliged to worship with the entire family. It is hard to listen long to the Word of God without hearing the rebuke of all such bitter feelings. For example, the very portion read, may say to the unrelenting one, "… if thou bring thy gift to the altar, and there rememberest that thy brother hath aught against thee, leave there thy gift before the altar, and go thy way; first be reconciled to thy brother, and then come and offer thy gift" (Matthew 5:23). At any rate, the whole spirit of the exercise convicts any family member who wishes to remain hard-hearted of his sin; for it is most difficult to pray with malice on the heart. The spirit of forgiveness often comes to us while we are upon our knees.

Suppose then, what we are reluctant to suppose, that mutual reproaches, perverse separation, and open quarrel, should enter a Christian family. To offenders, in such a case, the season of prayer must be an hour of keen rebuke. Avowedly, they are bowed down to pray for one another. The hypocrisy and impiety of attempting to do so out of a mind of hatred, will stare the sinner in the face, and will often bring him to repentance. Reconciliation, begun in the heart, during moments of devotion, may lead to the restoration of peace in the home.

Sad as is the thought, even husband and wife may be at odds with each other, and may give place to the devil. Harshness, severity, distrust, and unkindness, may spring up between those who have vowed to live together as heirs of the grace of life. But it is hard to believe that such persons, if they possess a spark of grace, can come to the posture and the words of prayer, encircled by their kneeling little ones, without surrendering the selfish spite, and making a faithful effort to crush the head of the viper. Marital tenderness, forbearance and love, are guarded by the exercises of family-devotion.

Contrast all this with the condition of a domestic circle subject to the same dark influences, but without these checks and this sacred balm, and you will no longer marvel that where there is no worship, there is no place for healing. The stream of unkindly temper runs on. Brooding silence is the best that can be expected. The day closes without reference to God. The griefs of the day are carried over into the morrow and all this because of a lack of spiritual influence that would be secured by the hour of prayer.

In speaking of family worship as a means of promoting family unity, we might dwell on its influence upon absent members of the household. As children grow up, there are few families that do not send forth from their bosom some children to distant places. These children are not forgotten at the hearth that they have left. Day by day, the venerable father, joined in silent love by the more melting mother, cries to God for him who is afar upon the sea, or in foreign lands. These are moments that bring the cherished object full before the mind, and make the absent one present to the heart. Such prayers serve many useful purposes. Chiefly, they rekindle and maintain the fire of affection. Most older children who leave home will not fail to prize these parental intercessions, or disregard the supplications of the brother or the sister left at home. Often, we are sure, the recollection of the domestic worship comes up before the distant youth, on the high seas, or in remote wanderings. Often is the secret tear shed over these privileges of his childhood. In the perpetual fire of the family altar, he knows that he has a stable refuge in his father's house.

When, after years of absence, which may be due to some sin, the son or daughter revisits the home of his childhood, and that worship is renewed which he remembers so well-what a torrent of ancient reminiscence pours into the heart! Such associations have their influence on even hardened natures, and they go to prove the blessedness of this familiar institution.

But after all that we may urge, the great and crowning reason why domestic worship promotes harmony, is, that it promotes true religion, and religion is love. Its mission is peace on earth and good will to men. Unlike the humanistic schemes of secular philosophers and psychologists, which tear the household elements asunder, Christianity compacts the structure, and strengthens every wall. It adds a new cement, and makes the father more a father—the mother more a mother—the son more a son; so that there is not a social tie which does not become more strong and endearing by means of grace. If even enemies are reduced to toleration by the gospel, how much greater must be its influence on the ties of blood and affinity! It consecrates every natural relation, and exalts human affections by expanding them into eternity.

The daily lessons, constantly recurring in family worship, bear directly on this point. "Husbands, love your wives, even as Christ also loved the Church. Let the wife see that she reverence her husband. Fathers, provoke not your children to wrath. Children, obey your parents in all things, for this is well-pleasing unto the Lord. Servants, be obedient to them that are your masters according to the flesh, with fear and trembling, in singleness of your heart, as unto Christ. And ye masters, do the same things unto them, forbearing threatening, knowing that your Master also is in heaven. Love as brethren, be pitiful, be courteous. Honor all men. Be not forgetful to entertain strangers. Be kindly affectioned one to another, with brotherly love, in honor preferring one another. Let all bitterness, and wrath, and anger, and clamor, and evil-speaking, be put away from you, with all malice: and be ye kind one to another, tender-hearted, forgiving one another, even as God for Christ's sake hath forgiven you." Such are the touching accents of the

gospel in general, and of this institution in particular, familiarized to
every member of a Christian house, from their childhood. And what
the Word of God enjoins, the Spirit of grace produces in the heart,
where true religion finds entrance. Under the daily influence of such
motives, which drop as the rain and distill as the dew, the youthful
heart may be expected, in many cases, to receive the noblest charities of
a renewed nature.

Amidst all the imperfections of a fallen world, there have been
thousands of families, since the founding of the Church, which have
realized this ideal; and what spectacle on earth is more lovely? From the
very cradle, the infant lips are taught to lisp the name of God, and the
soft voices of childhood join in the daily praise. Brothers and sisters,
already brought by baptism within the pale of the visible church, grow
up with all the additional reasons for mutual attachment, which spring
from dedication to God. No day passes in which parents and children
do not compass God's altars. When the father and mother begin to
descend into the autumn of life, they behold their offspring prepared
to walk in their steps. There is a church in the house. When death
enters, it is to make but a brief separation; and eternity sees the whole
family in heaven, without exception or omission.

In cases where divorce or death have prematurely fractured the
husband–wife relationship, single parents have even more reason to
maintain family worship. A broken family can only be fixed by the re-
establishment of Christ as the covenant head of the home. And there is
no better or more meaningful way to acknowledge the Lordship of
Christ, the Good Shepherd, than through the instrument of the family
altar. Only Christ can fill the void left by a family circle that has been
broken by divorce or death.

The happiest family on earth will not always be so. The most smil-
ing circle will be in tears some day. All that I ask is, that you would
secure for yourselves and your children, a friend in that blessed
Redeemer, who will wipe all tears from your faces. Your families may
soon be scattered, and familiar voices may cease to echo within your
walls. The children in a household do not stay children long. They
quickly grow up and take off for college or careers. O see to it, that the
God of Bethel goes with them, that they set up an altar even on a dis-
tant shore, and sing the Lord's song in that foreign land. They may be
taken from this earth altogether, and leave you alone. O see to it, that

as one after another goes, it may be to their Father's house above, and to sing with heavenly voices, the song that they first learned from you, and that you often sang together here—the song of Moses and the Lamb. And if you be taken, and some of them be left, see to it, that you leave them the thankful assurance that you are gone to their Father and your Father, their God and your God. And, in the meanwhile, let your united worship be so frequent and so fervent, that when you are taken from their head, the one whose sad responsibility it is to take your place, as priest of that household, shall not be able to select a chapter or a psalm with which your living image and voice are not associated, and in which you, though dead, are not yet speaking to them. "And thus my heart's wish for you all is,

'When soon or late you reach that coast,
O'er life's rough ocean driven;
May you rejoice, no wanderer lost,
A family in heaven.' "

James W. Alexander
Reprinted from Thoughts on Family Worship © *1847*

Doxology

The Old Hundredth L. M.

Thomas Ken 1709

Louis Bourgeois, 1551

Praise God from whom all bless - ings flow;

Praise him, all crea-tures here be - low; Praise him a - bove, ye

heav'n - ly host: Praise Fa - ther, Son, and Ho - ly Ghost. A - MEN.

The Old Hundredth L. M.

Thomas Ken 1709

Louis Bourgeois, 1551

Praise God from whom all bless - ings flow; Praise him, all

crea - tures here be - low; Praise him a - bove, ye heav'n - ly host:

Praise Fa - ther, Son, and Ho - ly Ghost. A - MEN.

The Ten Commandments

AND God spake all these words, saying, I am the LORD thy God, which have brought thee out of the land of Egypt, out of the house of bondage.

I. Thou shalt have no other gods before me.

II. Thou shalt not make unto thee any graven image, or any likeness of any thing that is in heaven above, or that is in the earth beneath, or that is in the water under the earth: Thou shalt not bow down thyself to them, nor serve them: for I the LORD thy God am a jealous God, visiting the iniquity of the fathers upon the children unto the third and fourth generation of them that hate me; and shewing mercy unto thousands of them that love me, and keep my commandments.

III. Thou shalt not take the name of the LORD thy God in vain; for the LORD will not hold him guiltless that taketh his name in vain.

IV. Remember the sabbath day, to keep it holy. Six days shalt thou labour, and do all thy work: But the seventh day is the sabbath of the LORD thy God: in it thou shalt not do any work, thou, nor thy son, nor thy daughter, thy manservant, nor thy maidservant, nor thy cattle, nor thy stranger that is within thy gates: For in six days the LORD made heaven and earth, the sea, and all that in them is, and rested the seventh day: wherefore the LORD blessed the sabbath day, and hallowed it.

V. Honour thy father and thy mother: that thy days may be long upon the land which the LORD thy God giveth thee.

VI. Thou shalt not kill.

VII. Thou shalt not commit adultery.

VIII. Thou shalt not steal.

IX. Thou shalt not bear false witness against thy neighbour.

X. Thou shalt not covet thy neighbour's house, thou shalt not covet thy neighbour's wife, nor his manservant, nor his maidservant, nor his ox, nor his ass, nor any thing that is thy neighbour's.

Exodus 20:1–17

The Greatest Commandments

HEAR also the words of our Lord Jesus, how He saith: "Thou shalt love the Lord thy God with all thy heart, and with all thy soul, and with all thy mind. This is the first and great commandment. And the second is like unto it, Thou shalt love thy neighbour as thyself. On these two commandments hang all the law and the prophets."

Matthew 22:37–40

Excerpts from the Apostles, Nicene, and Chalcedon Creeds

I believe in God the Father Almighty; and in Jesus Christ, His only Son, our Lord; truly God, and truly man, Light of Light, Very God of Very God; like unto us in all things, yet without sin; Who, for us men and our salvation, came down from heaven. He was conceived by the Holy Ghost; born of the Virgin Mary; crucified for us under Pontius Pilate, and suffered and was buried. The third day He rose again from the dead. He ascended into heaven and sitteth on the right hand of the Father. From thence He shall come to judge the quick and the dead. And I believe in the Holy Ghost, Who with the Father and the Son together is worshiped and glorified. And I believe in one holy and apostolic church, the communion of saints, the forgiveness of sins, the resurrection of the body, and the life everlasting. Amen.

The Lord's Prayer

Our Father which art in heaven, Hallowed be thy name. Thy kingdom come. Thy will be done in earth, as it is in heaven. Give us this day our daily bread. And forgive us our debts, as we forgive our debtors. And lead us not into temptation, but deliver us from evil: For thine is the kingdom, and the power, and the glory, for ever. Amen.

Matthew 6:9–13

Family Worship Hymnal

Hymns for Home and School

My Hope Is Built

EDWARD MOTE
WILLIAM B. BRADBURY

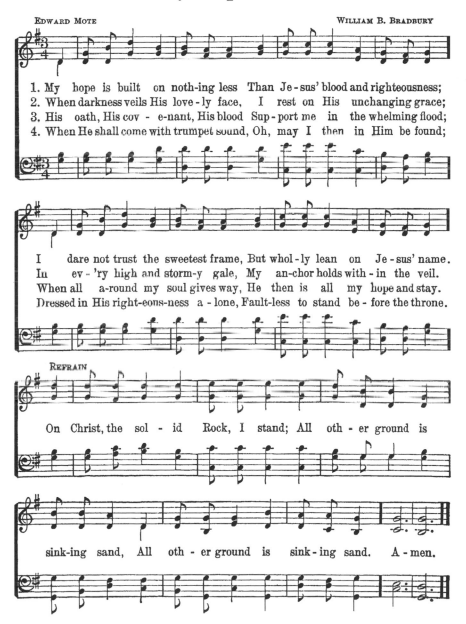

1. My hope is built on noth-ing less Than Je-sus' blood and righteousness;
2. When darkness veils His love-ly face, I rest on His unchanging grace;
3. His oath, His cov-e-nant, His blood Sup-port me in the whelming flood;
4. When He shall come with trumpet sound, Oh, may I then in Him be found;

I dare not trust the sweetest frame, But whol-ly lean on Je-sus' name.
In ev-'ry high and storm-y gale, My an-chor holds with-in the veil.
When all a-round my soul gives way, He then is all my hope and stay.
Dressed in His right-eous-ness a-lone, Fault-less to stand be-fore the throne.

REFRAIN

On Christ, the sol-id Rock, I stand; All oth-er ground is

sink-ing sand, All oth-er ground is sink-ing sand. A-men.

No Night There

John R. Clements.

H. P. Danks.

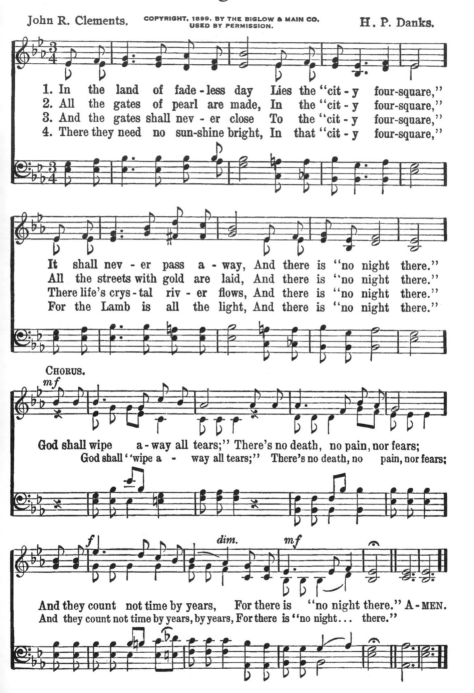

1. In the land of fade-less day Lies the "cit-y four-square,"
2. All the gates of pearl are made, In the "cit-y four-square,"
3. And the gates shall nev-er close To the "cit-y four-square,"
4. There they need no sun-shine bright, In that "cit-y four-square,"

It shall nev-er pass a-way, And there is "no night there."
All the streets with gold are laid, And there is "no night there."
There life's crys-tal riv-er flows, And there is "no night there."
For the Lamb is all the light, And there is "no night there."

CHORUS.

God shall wipe a-way all tears;" There's no death, no pain, nor fears;
God shall "wipe a - way all tears;" There's no death, no pain, nor fears;

And they count not time by years, For there is "no night there." A-MEN.
And they count not time by years, by years, For there is "no night... there."

Beneath the Cross of Jesus

Elizabeth C. Clephane

Frederick C. Maker

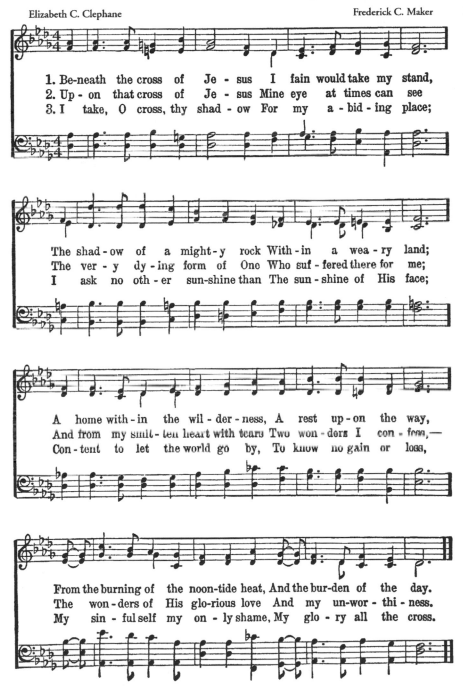

1. Be-neath the cross of Je - sus I fain would take my stand,
The shad-ow of a might-y rock With-in a wea-ry land;
A home with-in the wil-der-ness, A rest up-on the way,
From the burning of the noon-tide heat, And the bur-den of the day.

2. Up - on that cross of Je - sus Mine eye at times can see
The ver - y dy-ing form of One Who suf-fered there for me;
And from my smit-ten heart with tears Two won-ders I con - fess,—
The won-ders of His glo-rious love And my un-wor - thi - ness.

3. I take, O cross, thy shad-ow For my a-bid-ing place;
I ask no oth-er sun-shine than The sun-shine of His face;
Con-tent to let the world go by, To know no gain or loss,
My sin-ful self my on-ly shame, My glo-ry all the cross.

There Is a Heaven

Jessie Brown Pounds.   COPYRIGHT, 1919, BY E. O. EXCELL.   E. O. Excell.
                            WORDS AND MUSIC.

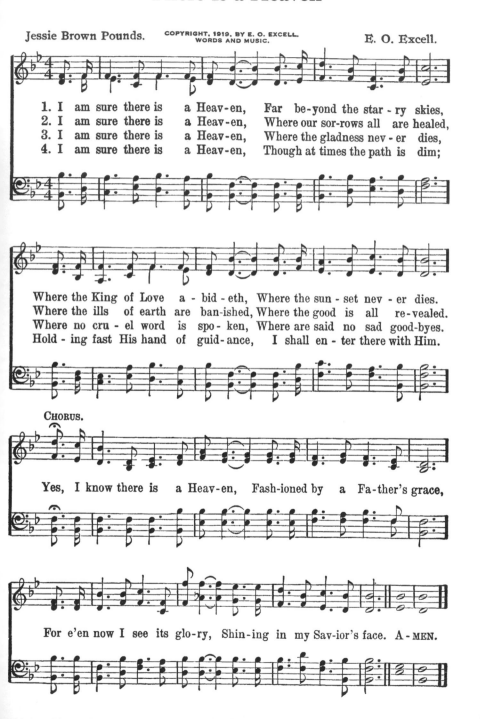

1. I am sure there is a Heav-en, Far be-yond the star - ry skies,
2. I am sure there is a Heav-en, Where our sor-rows all are healed,
3. I am sure there is a Heav-en, Where the gladness nev - er dies,
4. I am sure there is a Heav-en, Though at times the path is dim;

Where the King of Love a - bid - eth, Where the sun - set nev - er dies.
Where the ills of earth are ban-ished, Where the good is all re-vealed.
Where no cru - el word is spo- ken, Where are said no sad good-byes.
Hold - ing fast His hand of guid-ance, I shall en - ter there with Him.

CHORUS.

Yes, I know there is a Heav-en, Fash-ioned by a Fa-ther's grace,

For e'en now I see its glo-ry, Shin-ing in my Sav-ior's face. A - MEN.

Silent Night

P. M.

Franz Gruber

1. Si - lent night! ho - ly night! All is calm, all is bright 'Round yon
2. Si - lent night! ho - ly night! Shep - herds quake at the sight! Glo - ries
3. Si - lent night! ho - ly night! Son of God, love's pure light Ra - diant

vir - gin moth - er and Child! Ho - ly In - fant, so ten - der and mild,
stream from heaven a - far, Heav'n-ly hosts sing Al - le - lu - ia;
beams from Thy ho - ly face, With the dawn of re - deem - ing grace,

Sleep in heav - en - ly peace, Sleep in heav - en - ly peace.
Christ, the Sav - ior, is born, Christ, the Sav - ior, is born.
Je - sus, Lord, at Thy birth, Je - sus, Lord, at Thy birth. A- men.

A Child's Prayer

F. E. Belden

Griffith J. Jones

Andante

1. Guide and guard us, O our Fa - ther, Till an - oth - er Sab - bath day;
2. Now we thank Thee for Thy bless - ing On this sa - cred day of rest,

Shield us with Thy ho - ly pres-ence, Lead us in the right-eous way.
And for truths which Thou hast shown us, In Thy word di - vine - ly blest.

O Little Town of Bethlehem

PHILLIPS BROOKS　　　　　　　　　　　　　　　　　　　　LEWIS H. REDNER

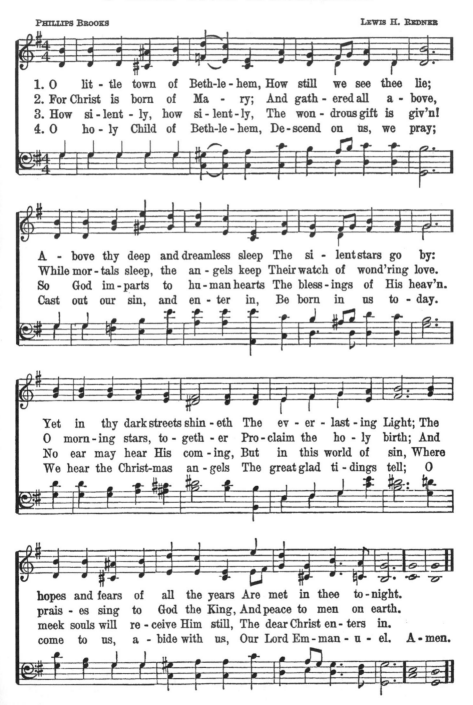

1. O lit-tle town of Beth-le-hem, How still we see thee lie;
2. For Christ is born of Ma-ry; And gath-ered all a-bove,
3. How si-lent-ly, how si-lent-ly, The won-drous gift is giv'n!
4. O ho-ly Child of Beth-le-hem, De-scend on us, we pray;

A-bove thy deep and dreamless sleep The si-lent stars go by:
While mor-tals sleep, the an-gels keep Their watch of wond'ring love.
So God im-parts to hu-man hearts The bless-ings of His heav'n.
Cast out our sin, and en-ter in, Be born in us to-day.

Yet in thy dark streets shin-eth The ev-er-last-ing Light; The
O morn-ing stars, to-geth-er Pro-claim the ho-ly birth; And
No ear may hear His com-ing, But in this world of sin, Where
We hear the Christ-mas an-gels The great glad ti-dings tell; O

hopes and fears of all the years Are met in thee to-night.
prais-es sing to God the King, And peace to men on earth.
meek souls will re-ceive Him still, The dear Christ en-ters in.
come to us, a-bide with us, Our Lord Em-man-u-el. A-men.

Do You Love Him?

T. O. Chisholm.

Henry P. Morton.

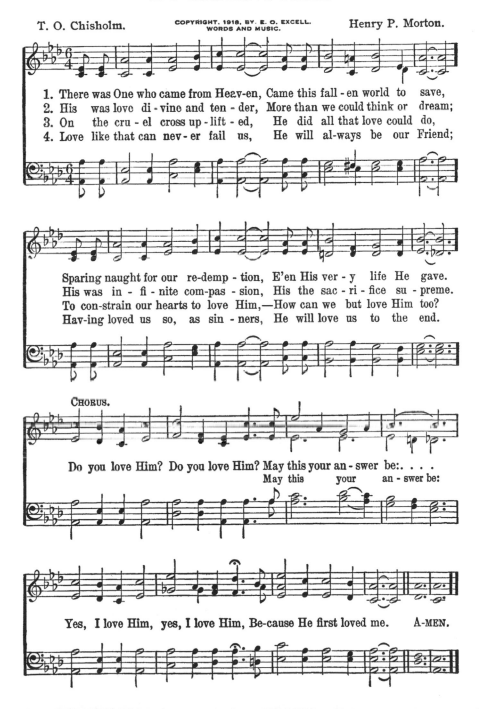

1. There was One who came from Heav-en, Came this fall - en world to save,
2. His was love di - vine and ten - der, More than we could think or dream;
3. On the cru - el cross up - lift - ed, He did all that love could do,
4. Love like that can nev - er fail us, He will al-ways be our Friend;

Sparing naught for our re-demp - tion, E'en His ver - y life He gave.
His was in - fi - nite com-pas - sion, His the sac - ri - fice su - preme.
To con-strain our hearts to love Him,—How can we but love Him too?
Hav-ing loved us so, as sin - ners, He will love us to the end.

CHORUS.

Do you love Him? Do you love Him? May this your an - swer be:. . . .
May this your an - swer be:

Yes, I love Him, yes, I love Him, Be-cause He first loved me. A-MEN.

Pardon on Calvary

Alfred Barratt.

Henry P. Morton.

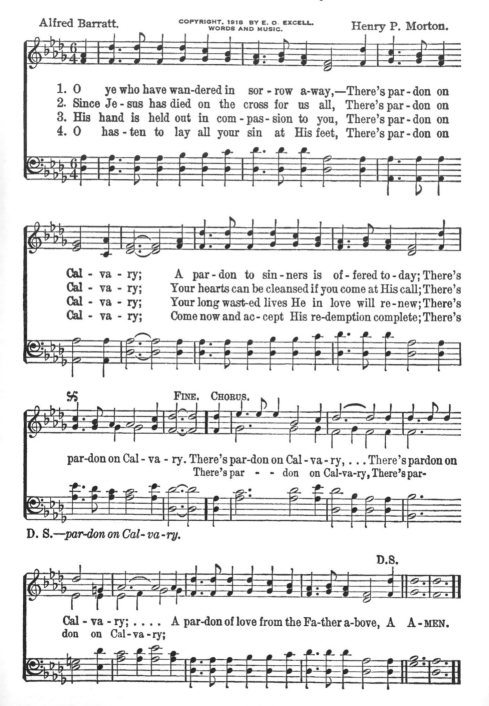

1. O ye who have wan-dered in sor-row a-way,—There's par-don on
2. Since Je-sus has died on the cross for us all, There's par-don on
3. His hand is held out in com-pas-sion to you, There's par-don on
4. O has-ten to lay all your sin at His feet, There's par-don on

Cal - va - ry;   A par-don to sin-ners is of-fered to-day; There's
Cal - va - ry;   Your hearts can be cleansed if you come at His call; There's
Cal - va - ry;   Your long wast-ed lives He in love will re-new; There's
Cal - va - ry;   Come now and ac-cept His re-demption complete; There's

FINE. CHORUS.

par-don on Cal-va-ry. There's par-don on Cal-va-ry, . . . There's pardon on
There's par - - don on Cal-va-ry, There's par-

D. S.—par-don on Cal-va-ry.

D.S.

Cal - va - ry; . . . . A par-don of love from the Fa-ther a-bove, A A - MEN.
don on Cal-va-ry;

He Lifted Me

Charlotte G. Homer.

Chas. H. Gabriel.

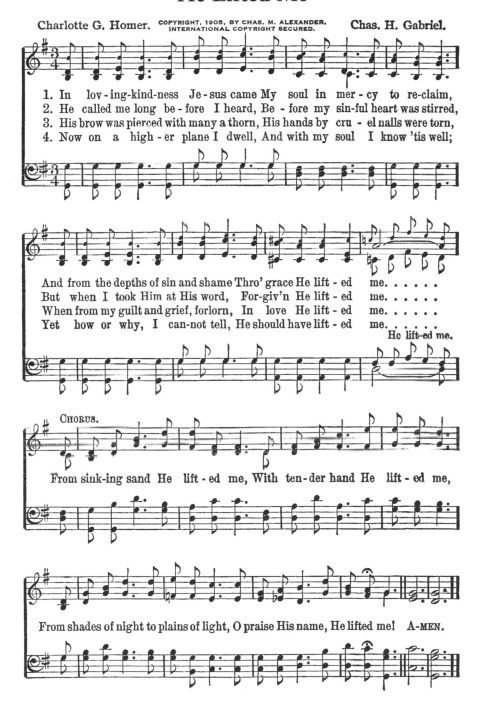

1. In lov-ing-kind-ness Je-sus came My soul in mer-cy to re-claim,
2. He called me long be-fore I heard, Be-fore my sin-ful heart was stirred,
3. His brow was pierced with many a thorn, His hands by cru-el nails were torn,
4. Now on a high-er plane I dwell, And with my soul I know 'tis well;

And from the depths of sin and shame Thro' grace He lift - ed me......
But when I took Him at His word, For-giv'n He lift - ed me......
When from my guilt and grief, forlorn, In love He lift - ed me......
Yet how or why, I can-not tell, He should have lift - ed me......

He lift-ed me.

CHORUS.

From sink-ing sand He lift - ed me, With ten-der hand He lift - ed me,

From shades of night to plains of light, O praise His name, He lifted me! A-MEN.

Beyond Our Sight

T. O. Chisholm.

Henry P. Morton.

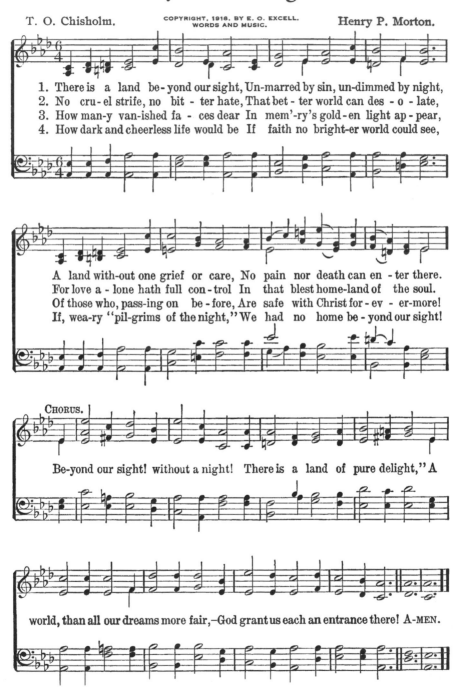

1. There is a land be-yond our sight, Un-marred by sin, un-dimmed by night,
2. No cru-el strife, no bit-ter hate, That bet-ter world can des-o-late,
3. How man-y van-ished fa-ces dear In mem'-ry's gold-en light ap-pear,
4. How dark and cheerless life would be If faith no bright-er world could see,

A land with-out one grief or care, No pain nor death can en-ter there.
For love a-lone hath full con-trol In that blest home-land of the soul.
Of those who, pass-ing on be-fore, Are safe with Christ for-ev-er-more!
If, wea-ry "pil-grims of the night," We had no home be-yond our sight!

CHORUS.

Be-yond our sight! without a night! There is a land of pure delight," A

world, than all our dreams more fair,—God grant us each an entrance there! A-MEN.

Everybody Should Know

Mrs. Frank A. Breck.

E. O. Excell.

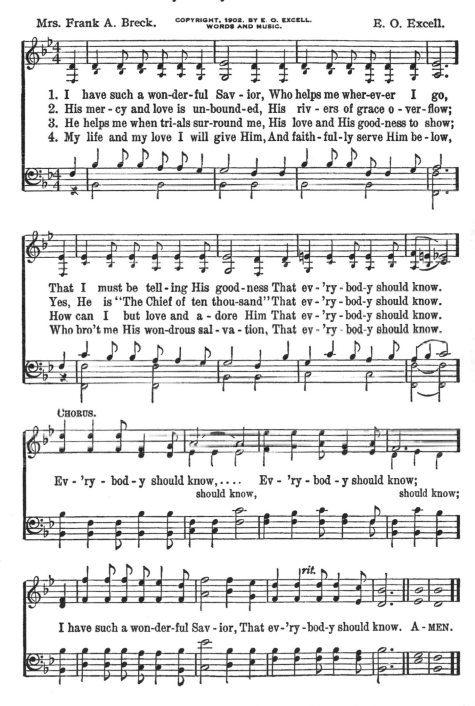

1. I have such a won-der-ful Sav - ior, Who helps me wher-ev-er I go,
2. His mer - cy and love is un-bound-ed, His riv - ers of grace o - ver-flow;
3. He helps me when tri-als sur-round me, His love and His good-ness to show;
4. My life and my love I will give Him, And faith-ful-ly serve Him be - low,

That I must be tell-ing His good-ness That ev-'ry-bod-y should know.
Yes, He is "The Chief of ten thou-sand" That ev-'ry-bod-y should know.
How can I but love and a - dore Him That ev-'ry-bod-y should know.
Who bro't me His won-drous sal-va-tion, That ev-'ry-bod-y should know.

CHORUS.

Ev-'ry-bod-y should know,.... Ev-'ry-bod-y should know;
should know, should know;

I have such a won-der-ful Sav - ior, That ev-'ry-bod-y should know. A-MEN.

There Shall Be Showers of Blessing

El Nathan.   James McGranahan.

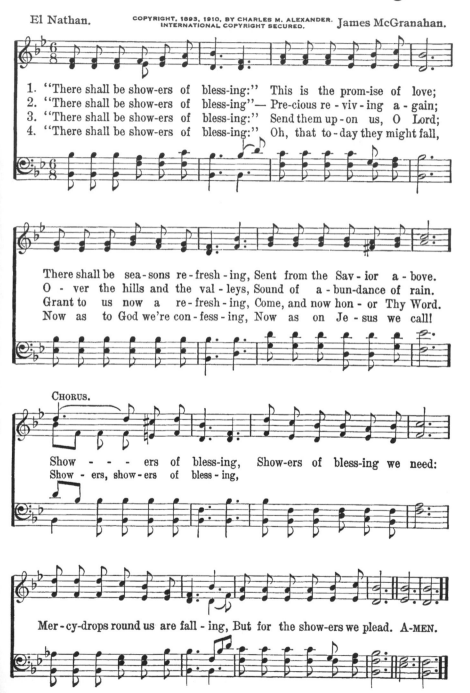

1. "There shall be show-ers of bless-ing:" This is the prom-ise of love;
2. "There shall be show-ers of bless-ing"— Pre-cious re-viv-ing a-gain;
3. "There shall be show-ers of bless-ing:" Send them up-on us, O Lord;
4. "There shall be show-ers of bless-ing:" Oh, that to-day they might fall,

There shall be sea-sons re-fresh-ing, Sent from the Sav-ior a-bove.
O-ver the hills and the val-leys, Sound of a-bun-dance of rain.
Grant to us now a re-fresh-ing, Come, and now hon-or Thy Word.
Now as to God we're con-fess-ing, Now as on Je-sus we call!

Chorus.

Show - - - ers of bless-ing, Show-ers of bless-ing we need:
Show - ers, show-ers of bless-ing,

Mer-cy-drops round us are fall-ing, But for the show-ers we plead. A-MEN.

Precious Promise

Nathaniel Niles.

P. P. Bliss.

1. Pre-cious prom-ise God hath giv-en To the wear-y pass-er-by,
2. When temp-ta-tions al-most win thee, And thy trust-ed watch-ers fly,
3. When thy se-cret hopes have perished In the grave of years gone by,
4. When the shades of life are fall-ing, And the hour has come to die,

On the way from earth to Heav-en, "I will guide thee with Mine eye."
Let this prom-ise ring with-in thee, "I will guide thee with Mine eye."
Let this prom-ise still be cher-ished, "I will guide thee with Mine eye."
Hear the trust-y Pi-lot call-ing, "I will guide thee with Mine eye."

CHORUS.

I will guide thee, I will guide thee, I will guide thee with Mine eye;

On the way from earth to Heav-en, I will guide thee with Mine eye. A-MEN.

Saved by Grace

Fanny J. Crosby.

Geo. C. Stebbins.

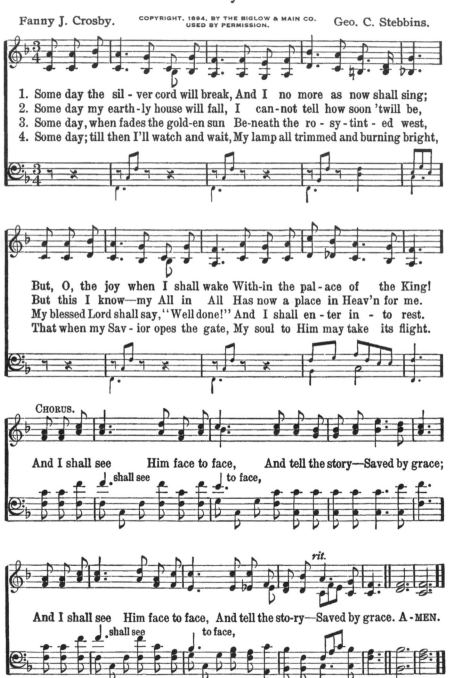

1. Some day the sil-ver cord will break, And I no more as now shall sing;
2. Some day my earth-ly house will fall, I can-not tell how soon 'twill be,
3. Some day, when fades the gold-en sun Be-neath the ro-sy-tint-ed west,
4. Some day; till then I'll watch and wait, My lamp all trimmed and burning bright,

But, O, the joy when I shall wake With-in the pal-ace of the King!
But this I know—my All in All Has now a place in Heav'n for me.
My blessed Lord shall say, "Well done!" And I shall en-ter in-to rest.
That when my Sav-ior opes the gate, My soul to Him may take its flight.

CHORUS.

And I shall see Him face to face, And tell the story—Saved by grace;
shall see to face,

And I shall see Him face to face, And tell the sto-ry—Saved by grace. A-MEN.
shall see to face,

Sweeter Than All

Johnson Oatman, Jr.

J. Howard Entwisle.

1. Christ will me His aid af-ford, Nev-er to fall, nev-er to fall;
2. I can fol-low all the way, Hear-ing Him call, hear-ing Him call;
3. Though a ves-sel I may be, Bro-ken and small, bro-ken and small,
4. When I reach the crys-tal sea, Voi-ces will call, voi-ces will call;

While I find my pre-cious Lord Sweet-er than all, sweet-er than all.
Find-ing Him from day to day, Sweet-er than all, sweet-er than all.
Yet His bless-ings fall on me, Sweet-er than all, sweet-er than all.
But my Sav-ior's voice will be Sweet-er than all, sweet-er than all.

CHORUS.

Je-sus is now, and ev-er will be, Sweet-er than all the world to me,

Since I heard His lov-ing call, Sweeter than all, sweeter than all. A-MEN.

Tell It Wherever You Go

Rev. Johnson Oatman, Jr.   COPYRIGHT, 1907, BY CHAS. H. GABRIEL. OWNED BY CHAS. REIGN SCOVILLE.   Wm. Edie Marks.

1. If Christ the Redeemer has pardoned your sin, Tell it wher-ev-er you go;
2. If now you are happy with Christ as your Guide, Tell it wher-ev-er you go;
3. When troubles assail do you trust in Him still? Tell it wher-ev-er you go;
4. If you are an heir to a man-sion on high, Tell it wher-ev-er you go;

If in-to your darkness His light has shown in, Tell it wher-ev-er you go.
If He is your Friend, and with Him you abide, Tell it wher-ev-er you go.
When sorrows o'erwhelm do you sink in His will, Tell it wher-ev-er you go.
Un-til you find rest in that home in the sky, Tell it wher-ev-er you go.

CHORUS.

Tell it, ... tell it, ... Tell it wher-ev-er you go; If
Tell it that oth-ers a-round you may know,

you would win others from sin and from woe, Tell it wher-ev-er you go!   A-MEN.

All in All to Me

C. H. G.

Chas. H. Gabriel.

1. All in all to me is Je-sus! Ev - 'ry need His grace supplies;
2. All in all to me is Je-sus, Lord, Redeemer, Sav-ior, Friend;
3. All in all to me is Je-sus, Bless-ed One of Cal-va-ry;
4. All in all to me is Je-sus, I am His, and He is mine;

Day by day He guides and keeps me,— No good thing to me de - nies.
Ten-der Shepherd, He will guard me, And from ev-'ry foe de - fend.
I will nev-er cease to love Him Who has done so much for me.
To His love, and in His serv-ice, Ev - 'ry-thing I now re - sign.

CHORUS.

In His love I am a - bid-ing; Ev-'ry-thing to Him con - fid-ing;

'Neath His wing my soul is hid-ing, He is all in all to me. A-MEN.

Wonderful Jesus

Rev. W. J. Stuart.   COPYRIGHT, 1909, BY E. O. EXCELL.   Jno. R. Sweney.
                                    WORDS AND MUSIC.

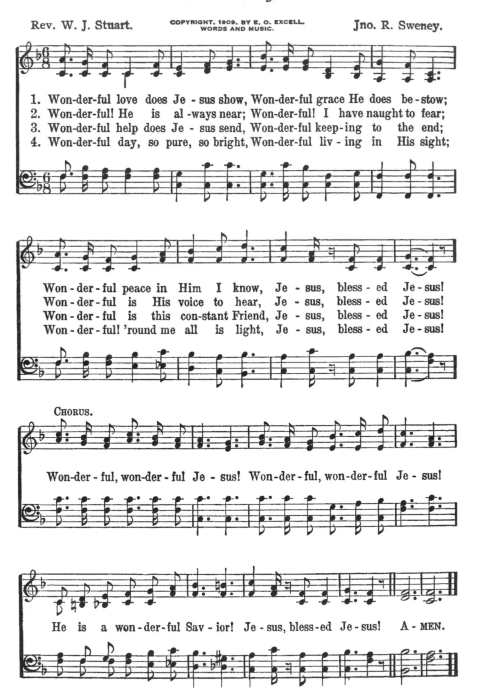

1. Won-der-ful love does Je - sus show, Won-der-ful grace He does be - stow;
2. Won-der-ful! He is al -ways near; Won-der-ful! I have naught to fear;
3. Won-der-ful help does Je - sus send, Won-der-ful keep-ing to the end;
4. Won-der-ful day, so pure, so bright, Won-der-ful liv - ing in His sight;

Won - der - ful peace in Him I know, Je - sus, bless - ed Je - sus!
Won - der - ful is His voice to hear, Je - sus, bless - ed Je - sus!
Won - der - ful is this con-stant Friend, Je - sus, bless - ed Je - sus!
Won - der - ful! 'round me all is light, Je - sus, bless - ed Je - sus!

CHORUS.

Won-der - ful, won-der - ful Je - sus! Won-der - ful, won-der-ful Je - sus!

He is a won-der-ful Sav - ior! Je - sus, bless-ed Je - sus! A - MEN.

Day is Dying in the West

Mary A. Lathbury   *Evening Praise. 7s. 4.*   William F. Sherwin.

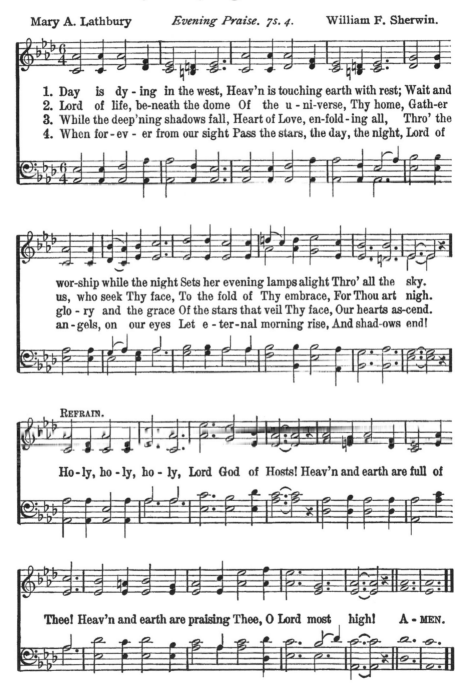

1. Day is dy-ing in the west, Heav'n is touching earth with rest; Wait and
2. Lord of life, be-neath the dome Of the u-ni-verse, Thy home, Gath-er
3. While the deep'ning shadows fall, Heart of Love, en-fold-ing all, Thro' the
4. When for-ev-er from our sight Pass the stars, the day, the night, Lord of

wor-ship while the night Sets her evening lamps alight Thro' all the sky.
us, who seek Thy face, To the fold of Thy embrace, For Thou art nigh.
glo-ry and the grace Of the stars that veil Thy face, Our hearts as-cend.
an-gels, on our eyes Let e-ter-nal morning rise, And shad-ows end!

REFRAIN.

Ho-ly, ho-ly, ho-ly, Lord God of Hosts! Heav'n and earth are full of

Thee! Heav'n and earth are praising Thee, O Lord most high! A-MEN.

Whom, Having Not Seen, I Love

Maud Frazer.

Chas. H. Gabriel.

1. A Friend have I who stand-eth near, To com-fort me and still each fear;
2. In vain may fan-cy strive to trace My Sav-ior's beau-ty and His grace;
3. The pre-cious hope I have each day Il-lu-mines all my earth-ly way,
4. With that fair man-sion e'er in view, My pil-grim jour-ney I pur-sue,

It is my Lord and Sav-ior dear, Whom, hav-ing not seen, I love.
More fair than I can dream, His face, Whom, hav-ing not seen, I love.
That He will take me home to stay, Whom, hav-ing not seen, I love.
And try my Sav-ior's will to do, Whom, hav-ing not seen, I love.

CHORUS.

And He is pre-par-ing a place...... For me in His home a-bove,..
And He is pre-par-ing a place For me in His home a-bove,

Where I shall be-hold His face,... Whom, having not seen, I love. A-MEN.
Where I........ shall be-hold His face,

God Will Take Care of You

C. D. Martin.　　　COPYRIGHT, 1905, BY JOHN A. DAVIS.　　W. S. Martin.
　　　　　　　　　　　USED BY PERMISSION.

1. Be not dis-mayed, what-e'er be-tide, God will take care of you;
2. Thro' days of toil, when heart doth fail, God will take care of you;
3. All you may need He will pro-vide, God will take care of you;
4. No mat-ter what may be the test, God will take care of you;

Be-neath His wings of love a-bide, God will take care of you.
When dan-gers fierce your path as-sail, God will take care of you.
Noth-ing you ask will be de-nied, God will take care of you.
Lean, wear-y one, up-on His breast, God will take care of you.

CHORUS.

God will take care of you, Thro' ev-'ry day, O'er all the way;

He will take care of you, God will take care of you. . . A-MEN.
take care of you.

Near the Cross

Fanny J. Crosby.

W. H. Doane.

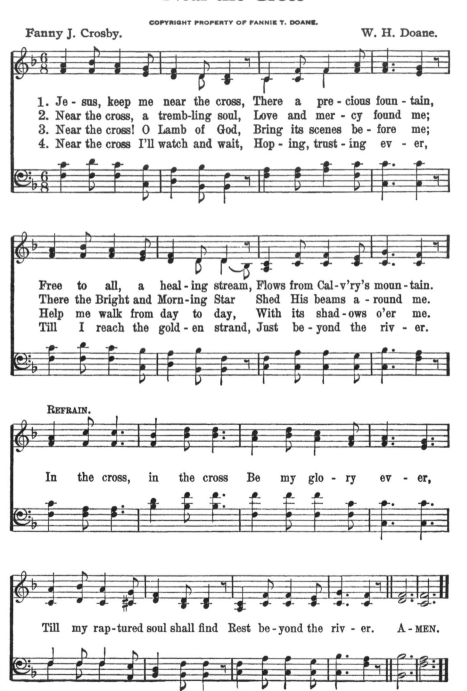

1. Je - sus, keep me near the cross, There a pre - cious foun - tain,
2. Near the cross, a tremb-ling soul, Love and mer - cy found me;
3. Near the cross! O Lamb of God, Bring its scenes be - fore me;
4. Near the cross I'll watch and wait, Hop - ing, trust - ing ev - er,

Free to all, a heal - ing stream, Flows from Cal-v'ry's moun - tain.
There the Bright and Morn-ing Star Shed His beams a - round me.
Help me walk from day to day, With its shad-ows o'er me.
Till I reach the gold - en strand, Just be - yond the riv - er.

REFRAIN.

In the cross, in the cross Be my glo - ry ev - er,

Till my rap-tured soul shall find Rest be-yond the riv - er. A - MEN.

My Savior's Love

C. H. G.   Chas. H. Gabriel.

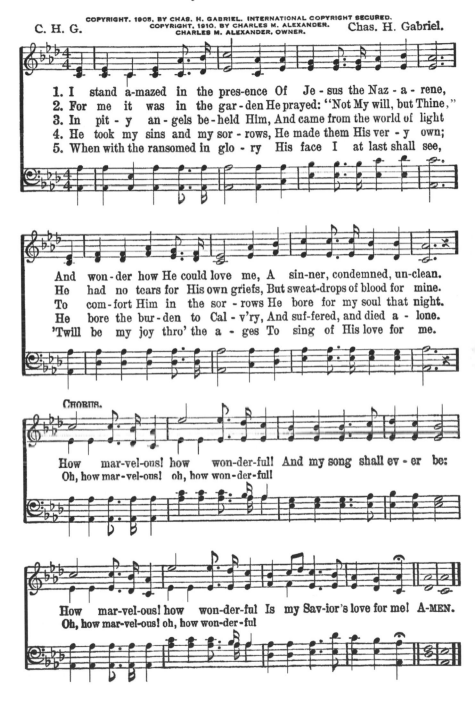

1. I stand a-mazed in the pres-ence Of Je-sus the Naz-a-rene,
2. For me it was in the gar-den He prayed: "Not My will, but Thine,"
3. In pit-y an-gels be-held Him, And came from the world of light
4. He took my sins and my sor-rows, He made them His ver-y own;
5. When with the ransomed in glo-ry His face I at last shall see,

And won-der how He could love me, A sin-ner, condemned, un-clean.
He had no tears for His own griefs, But sweat-drops of blood for mine.
To com-fort Him in the sor-rows He bore for my soul that night.
He bore the bur-den to Cal-v'ry, And suf-fered, and died a-lone.
'Twill be my joy thro' the a-ges To sing of His love for me.

Chorus.

How mar-vel-ous! how won-der-ful! And my song shall ev-er be:
Oh, how mar-vel-ous! oh, how won-der-ful!

How mar-vel-ous! how won-der-ful Is my Sav-ior's love for me! A-MEN.
Oh, how mar-vel-ous! oh, how won-der-ful

Jesus Is the Friend You Need

I. E. R. COPYRIGHT, 1918, BY ROBERT H. COLEMAN. I. E. Reynolds.

1. When the sun shines bright and your heart is light, Je-sus is the Friend you need;
2. If you're lost in sin, all is dark with-in, Je-sus is the Friend you need;
3. When in that sad hour, when in death's grim pow'r, Je-sus is the Friend you need;
4. When the cares of life all a-round are rife, Je-sus is the Friend you need;

When the clouds hang low in this world of woe, Je-sus is the Friend you need.
God a-lone can save thro' the Son He gave, Je-sus is the Friend you need.
If you would prepare 'gainst the tempter's snare, Je-sus is the Friend you need.
Glo-ry to His name, al-ways He's the same, Je-sus is the Friend you need.

CHORUS.

Je-sus is the Friend you need, Such a Friend is He in-
Je - - sus is the Friend you need, Such a

deed; He who no-teth ev-'ry tear, He will
Friend is He in-deed;

ban-ish ev-'ry fear, Je-sus is the Friend you need. A-MEN.

Take the Name of Jesus with You

Mrs. Lydia Baxter. COPYRIGHT, 1899, BY W. H. DOANE. RENEWAL. W. H. Doane.

1. Take the name of Je-sus with you, Child of sor-row and of woe;
2. Take the name of Je-sus ev - er As a shield from ev-'ry snare;
3. O the pre-cious name of Je - sus! How it thrills our souls with joy,
4. At the name of Je-sus bow - ing, Fall-ing pros-trate at His feet,

It will joy and com-fort give you, Take it then, wher-e'er you go.
If temp-ta-tions round you gath - er, Breathe that ho - ly name in prayer
When His lov-ing arms re - ceive us, And His songs our tongues employ!
King of kings in Heav'n we'll crown Him, When our jour-ney is com-plete.

CHORUS.

Pre - cious name, O how sweet!
Pre-cious name, O how sweet!
Hope of earth and joy of Heav'n; Pre - cious name,
Pre-cious name, O how
O how sweet! . . . Hope of earth and joy of Heav'n. A - MEN.
sweet, how sweet!

Grace, Enough for Me

E. O. E.

E. O. Excell.

1. In look-ing thro' my tears one day, I saw Mount Cal-va-ry; Be-neath the cross there flowed a stream Of grace, e-nough for me.
2. While standing there, my trem-bling heart, Once full of ag-o-ny, Could scarce be-lieve the sight I saw Of grace, e-nough for me.
3. When I be-held my ev-'ry sin Nailed to the cru-el tree, I felt a flood go thro' my soul Of grace, e-nough for me.
4. When I am safe with-in the veil, My por-tion there will be, To sing thro' all the years to come Of grace, e-nough for me.

CHORUS.

Grace is flow-ing from Cal-va-ry, ... Grace as fath-om-less as the sea, .. Grace for time and e-ter-ni-ty, ... Grace, .. e-nough for me.

e-nough for me. Grace is flow-ing from Cal-va-ry for me, Grace as fath-om-less as the roll-ing sea, Grace for time and e-ter-ni-ty, His a-bun-dant grace I see, e-nough for me. A-MEN.

Growing Dearer Each Day

C. H. G.

Chas. H. Gabriel.

1. How sweet is the love of my Sav-ior! 'Tis boundless and deep as the sea; And
2. I know He is ev-er be-side me! E - ter - ni-ty on-ly will prove The
3. Wher-ev-er He leads I will fol-low, Thro' sor-row, or shadow, or sun; And
4. Some day face to face I shall see Him, And oh, what a joy it will be To

best of it all, it is dai-ly Grow-ing sweet-er and sweet-er to me.
height and the depth of His mercy, And the breadth of His in-fi-nite love.
though I be tried in the fur-nace, I can say,"Lord, Thy will be it done."
know that His love, now so precious, Will for-ev - er grow sweet-er to me.

CHORUS.

Sweet - - er and sweeter to me, ... Dear - - er and
Sweeter to me, grow - ing sweet-er to me, Dear-er each day,

dear-er each day; . . . Oh, won - - der-ful love of my
grow - ing dear-er each day; Oh, won-der-ful love, love of my

Sav - ior, Grow-ing dear - - er each step of my way! A - MEN.
Sav - ior, Grow-ing dear-er and dear-er each step of my way!

Christ Receiveth Sinful Men

Arr. from Neumaster, 1671.   James McGranahan.

1. Sin - ners Je - sus will re - ceive: Sound this word of grace to all
2. Come, and He will give you rest; Trust Him, for His word is plain;
3. Now my heart condemns me not, Pure be - fore the law I stand;
4. Christ re - ceiv - eth sin - ful men, E - ven me with all my sin;

Who the heav'n-ly path-way leave, All who lin - ger, all who fall.
He will take the sin - ful - est; Christ re - ceiv - eth sin - ful men.
He who cleansed me from all spot, Sat - is - fied its last de - mand.
Purged from ev - 'ry spot and stain, Heav'n with Him I en - ter in.

REFRAIN.

Sing it o'er. . . . . . and o'er a - gain;. . . . . . Christ re-
Sing it o'er a - gain,   Sing it o'er a - gain; Christ re-

ceiv - - - eth sin-ful men;. . . ;. . Make the mes - - - sage
ceiv -eth sin - ful men, Christ re - ceiv-eth sin - ful men;   Make the message plain,

clear and plain:. . . . . Christ re - ceiv - eth sin - ful men. A-MEN.
Make the message plain:

Send the Light

C. H. G. Chas. H. Gabriel.

1. There's a call comes ring-ing o'er the rest-less wave, "Send the light! . . .
2. We have heard the Mac - e - do - nian call to-day, "Send the light! . . .
3. Let us pray that grace may ev'ry-where a-bound; Send the light! . . .
4. Let us not grow wear - y in the work of love, Send the light! . . .

Send the light!

Send the light!" There are souls to res-cue, there are souls to save,
Send the light!" And a gold - en of-f'ring at the cross we lay,
Send the light! And a Christ-like spir - it ev - 'ry-where be found,
Send the light! Let us gath - er jew - els for a crown a - bove,

Send the light!

REFRAIN.

Send the light! . . . Send the light! . . . Send the light! . . . the
Send the light! Send the light! Send the light!

bless - ed gos - pel light; Let it shine . . . . from shore to
the bless - ed gos - pel light; Let it shine

shore! . . . . . shine . . . for-ev - er - more. . . . . . A-MEN.
from shore to shore! Let it shine for-ev - er-more.

We Shall See the King Some Day

He is so Precious to Me

C. H. G.

Chas. H. Gabriel.

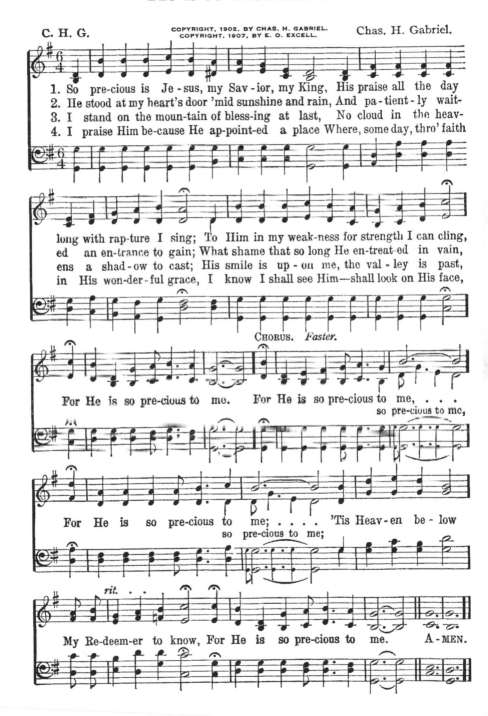

1. So pre-cious is Je-sus, my Sav-ior, my King, His praise all the day
2. He stood at my heart's door 'mid sunshine and rain, And pa-tient-ly wait-
3. I stand on the moun-tain of bless-ing at last, No cloud in the heav-
4. I praise Him be-cause He ap-point-ed a place Where, some day, thro' faith

long with rap-ture I sing; To Him in my weak-ness for strength I can cling,
ed an en-trance to gain; What shame that so long He en-treat-ed in vain,
ens a shad-ow to cast; His smile is up-on me, the val-ley is past,
in His won-der-ful grace, I know I shall see Him—shall look on His face,

CHORUS. Faster.

For He is so pre-cious to me. For He is so pre-cious to me, . . .
so pre-cious to me,

For He is so pre-cious to me; . . . . 'Tis Heav-en be-low
so pre-cious to me;

rit. . . .

My Re-deem-er to know, For He is so pre-cious to me. A-MEN.

As a Volunteer

W. S. Brown. COPYRIGHT, 1907, BY CHAS. H. GABRIEL. E. O. EXCELL, OWNER. Chas. H. Gabriel.

1. A call for loy-al sol-diers Comes to one and all; Sol-diers for the con-flict,
2. Yes, Jesus calls for soldiers Who are filled with pow'r, Soldiers who will serve Him
3. He calls you, for He loves you With a heart most kind, He whose heart was broken,
4. And when the war is o-ver, And the vic-t'ry won, When the true and faith-ful

Will you heed the call! Will you an-swer quick-ly, With a read-y cheer,
Ev-'ry day and hour; He will not for-sake you, He is ev-er near;
Bro-ken for man-kind; Now, just now He calls you, Calls in ac-cents clear,
Gath-er one by one, He will crown with glo-ry All who there ap-pear;

CHORUS.

Will you be en-list-ed As a vol-un-teer? A vol-un-teer for Je-sus, A sol-dier

true! Oth-ers have enlisted, Why not you? Je-sus is the Cap-tain,
O why not?

We will nev-er fear; Will you be en-list-ed As a vol-un-teer? A-MEN.

Only a Sinner

James M. Gray.   D. B. Towner.

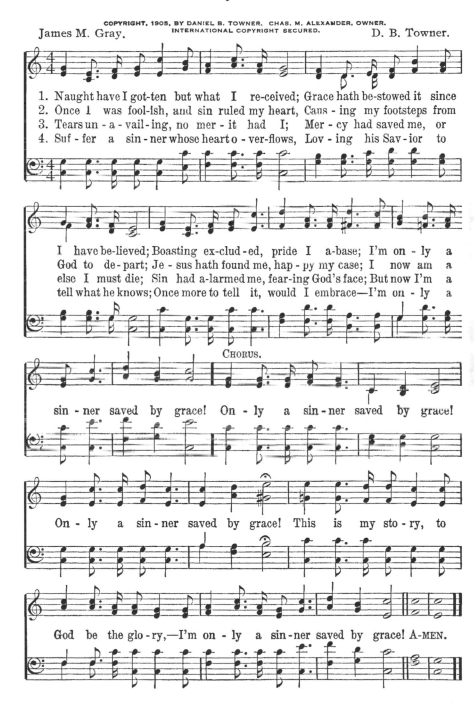

1. Naught have I got-ten but what I re-ceived; Grace hath be-stowed it since
2. Once I was fool-ish, and sin ruled my heart, Caus - ing my footsteps from
3. Tears un - a - vail-ing, no mer - it had I; Mer - cy had saved me, or
4. Suf - fer a sin - ner whose heart o - ver-flows, Lov - ing his Sav - ior to

I have be-lieved; Boasting ex-clud-ed, pride I a-base; I'm on - ly a
God to de-part; Je - sus hath found me, hap - py my case; I now am a
else I must die; Sin had a-larmed me, fear-ing God's face; But now I'm a
tell what he knows; Once more to tell it, would I embrace—I'm on - ly a

CHORUS.

sin - ner saved by grace! On - ly a sin - ner saved by grace!

On - ly a sin - ner saved by grace! This is my sto - ry, to

God be the glo - ry,—I'm on - ly a sin - ner saved by grace! A-MEN.

Spend One Hour with Jesus

Katharine A. Grimes.
E. O. Excell.

1. Wear-y soul by sin op-pressed, Spend one hour with Je-sus;
2. Do you fear the gath-'ring gloom? Spend one hour with Je-sus;
3. Ev-'ry need He will sup-ply, Spend one hour with Je-sus;
4. All a-long life's storm-y way, Spend one hour with Je-sus;

He will give your spir-it rest, Spend one hour with Je-sus:
In the si-lent in-ner room, Spend one hour with Je-sus:
He a-lone can sat-is-fy, Spend one hour with Je-sus:
Call up-on Him day by day, Spend one hour with Je-sus:

He has felt your grief be-fore, Num-bered all your sor-rows o'er,
He will speak un-to your soul, Make your ev-'ry heart-ache whole,
Oh, the mer-cy He will show, Oh, the grace He will be-stow,
Tell Him all— He is your Friend, He will count-less bless-ings send,

He will ev-'ry joy re-store; Spend one hour with Je-sus.
Point you to the Heav'nly Goal; Spend one hour with Je-sus.
Grace to con-quer ev-'ry foe; Spend one hour with Je-sus.
He will keep you to the end; Spend one hour with Je-sus. A-MEN.

'Tis the Blessed Hour of Prayer

Fanny J. Crosby.

W. H. Doane.

1. 'Tis the bless-ed hour of prayer, when our hearts low-ly bend, And we
2. 'Tis the bless-ed hour of prayer, when the Sav-ior draws near, With a
3. 'Tis the bless-ed hour of prayer, when the tempt-ed and tried To the
4. At the bless-ed hour of prayer, trust-ing Him, we be-lieve That the

gath-er to Je-sus, our Sav-ior and Friend; If we come to Him in
ten-der com-pas-sion His chil-dren to hear; When He tells us we may
Sav-ior who loves them their sor-row con-fide; With a sym-pa-thiz-ing
bless-ing we're need-ing we'll sure-ly re-ceive; In the full-ness of this

faith, His pro-tec-tion to share, What a balm for the wear-y!
cast at His feet ev-'ry care, What a balm for the wear-y!
heart He re-moves ev-'ry care; What a balm for the wear-y!
trust we shall lose ev-'ry care; What a balm for the wear-y!

CHORUS.

O how sweet to be there! Bless-ed hour of prayer, bless-ed hour of

prayer, What a balm for the wear-y! O how sweet to be there! A-MEN.

We're Marching to Zion

Isaac Watts.

Robert Lowry.

1. Come, we that love the Lord, And let our joys be known; Join
2. Let those re - fuse to sing Who nev - er knew our God; But
3. The hill of Zi - on yields A thou-sand sa - cred sweets, Be-
4. Then let our songs a-bound, And ev - 'ry tear be dry; We're

in a song with sweet ac - cord, Join in a song with sweet ac - cord,
chil - dren of the heav'n-ly King, But chil - dren of the heav'n-ly King,
fore we reach the heav'nl-y fields, Be - fore we reach the heav'n-ly fields,
marching thro' Im-man-uel's ground, We're marching thro' Immanuel's ground,

And thus sur - round the throne, And thus sur-round the throne.
May speak their joys a-broad, May speak their joys a - broad.
Or walk the gold - en streets, Or walk the gold-en streets.
To fair - er worlds on high, To fair - er worlds on high.
(1) And thus sur-round the throne, And thus sur-round the throne.

CHORUS.

We're march - ing to Zi - on, Beau - ti - ful, beau-ti-ful Zi - on; We're
We're march-ing on to Zi - on,

march-ing up-ward to Zi - on, The beau-ti-ful cit-y of God. A - MEN.
Zi - on, Zi - on,

I've Found a Friend

J. G. Small.

Geo. C Stebbins.

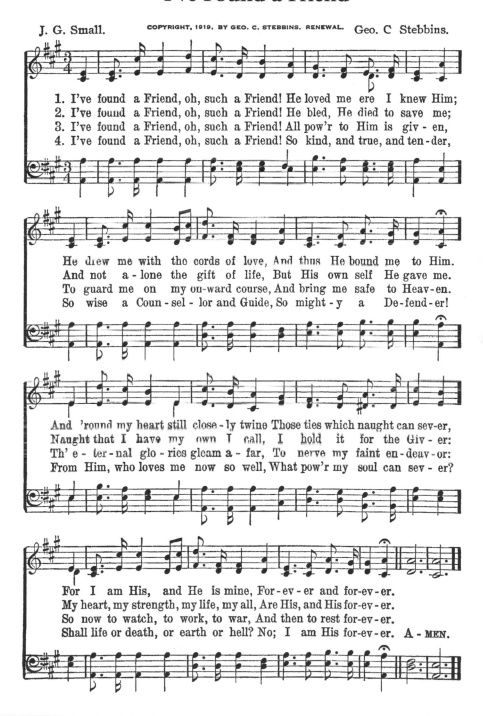

1. I've found a Friend, oh, such a Friend! He loved me ere I knew Him;
2. I've found a Friend, oh, such a Friend! He bled, He died to save me;
3. I've found a Friend, oh, such a Friend! All pow'r to Him is giv - en,
4. I've found a Friend, oh, such a Friend! So kind, and true, and ten-der,

He drew me with the cords of love, And thus He bound me to Him.
And not a - lone the gift of life, But His own self He gave me.
To guard me on my on-ward course, And bring me safe to Heav-en.
So wise a Coun - sel - lor and Guide, So might - y a De-fend-er!

And 'round my heart still close - ly twine Those ties which naught can sev-er,
Naught that I have my own I call, I hold it for the Giv - er:
Th' e - ter-nal glo - ries gleam a - far, To nerve my faint en-deav-or:
From Him, who loves me now so well, What pow'r my soul can sev - er?

For I am His, and He is mine, For - ev - er and for-ev - er.
My heart, my strength, my life, my all, Are His, and His for-ev - er.
So now to watch, to work, to war, And then to rest for-ev - er.
Shall life or death, or earth or hell? No; I am His for-ev - er. A - MEN.

I Know That He is Nigh

Rev. John A. Stover. Rev. Clarence McDaniels.

1. When the storms of life are rag-ing, And the bil-lows toss me high,
2. When the tempter's darts as-sail me, And I see my cour-age die,
3. When the sun is shin-ing on me, Or the dark clouds fill the sky,
4. Then I sing for I am hap-py, And my joy can nev-er die,

It is then my Sav-ior holds me, For I know that He is nigh;..
I then reach a hand to Je-sus, And He saves me for He's nigh;..
There is not a thing can harm me, For my Sav-ior's al-ways nigh;..
For my Sav-ior walks be-side me, And I know He's al-ways nigh;..

Nigh to qui-et ev-'ry bil-low, Nigh the tem-pest to de-stroy,....
Nigh to qui-et ev-'ry pas-sion, Nigh their glamour to de-stroy,....
Nigh to shield me when in dan-ger, Nigh the shad-ows to de-stroy,....
Nigh to help me on my jour-ney, Nigh death's power to de-stroy,....

Nigh to keep my heart from fainting, And to fill my soul with joy.
Nigh to keep my heart from fainting, And to fill my soul with joy.
Nigh to keep my heart from fainting, And to fill my soul with joy.
Nigh to keep my heart from fainting, And to fill my soul with joy. A-MEN.

Jesus is All the World to Me

W. L. T.

COPYRIGHT, 1904, BY WILL L. THOMPSON.
HOPE PUBLISHING CO., OWNER.

Will L. Thompson.

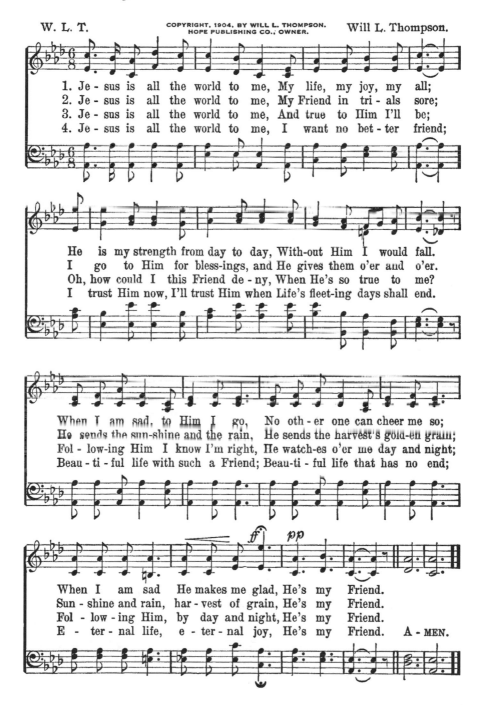

1. Je - sus is all the world to me, My life, my joy, my all;
2. Je - sus is all the world to me, My Friend in tri - als sore;
3. Je - sus is all the world to me, And true to Him I'll be;
4. Je - sus is all the world to me, I want no bet - ter friend;

He is my strength from day to day, With-out Him I would fall.
I go to Him for bless-ings, and He gives them o'er and o'er.
Oh, how could I this Friend de - ny, When He's so true to me?
I trust Him now, I'll trust Him when Life's fleet-ing days shall end.

When I am sad, to Him I go, No oth - er one can cheer me so;
He sends the sun-shine and the rain, He sends the harvest's gold-en grain;
Fol - low-ing Him I know I'm right, He watch-es o'er me day and night;
Beau - ti - ful life with such a Friend; Beau-ti - ful life that has no end;

When I am sad He makes me glad, He's my Friend.
Sun - shine and rain, har - vest of grain, He's my Friend.
Fol - low - ing Him, by day and night, He's my Friend.
E - ter - nal life, e - ter - nal joy, He's my Friend. A - MEN.

Safely Through Another Week

John Newton.   *Sabbath. 7s.*   Lowell Mason.

1. Safe - ly through an - oth - er week God has brought us on our way;
2. While we pray for par-d'ning grace, Thro' the dear Re-deem-er's name,
3. Here we come Thy name to praise, Let us feel Thy pres-ence near;
4. May Thy gos-pel's joy - ful sound Con - quer sin-ners, com-fort saints;

Let us now a bless-ing seek, Wait-ing in His courts to - day;
Show Thy rec - on - cil - ed face; Take a - way our sin and shame:
May Thy glo - ry meet our eyes, While we in Thy house ap - pear:
Make the fruits of grace a - bound, Bring re - lief for all com-plaints:

Day of all the week the best, Em-blem of e - ter - nal rest: Day of
From our world-ly cares set free, May we rest this day in Thee: From our
Here af - ford us, Lord, a taste Of our ev - er - last-ing feast: Here af-
Thus may all our Sab-baths prove, Till we join the Church a - bove: Thus may

all the week the best, Em-blem of e - ter - nal rest.
world-ly cares set free, May we rest this day in Thee.
ford us, Lord, a taste Of our ev - er - last-ing feast.
all our Sab-baths prove, Till we join the Church a - bove. A - MEN.

O Day of Rest and Gladness

C. Wordsworth.   *Mendebras. 7s. 6s. D.*   Arr. by L. Mason.

1. O day of rest and glad-ness, O day of joy and light,
2. On thee, at the cre-a-tion, The light first had its birth;
3. To-day on wear-y na-tions The heav'n-ly man-na falls;
4. New gra-ces ev-er gain-ing From this our day of rest,

O balm of care and sad-ness, Most beau-ti-ful, most bright;
On thee, for our sal-va-tion, Christ rose from depths of earth.
To ho-ly con-vo-ca-tions The sil-ver trump-et calls,
We reach the rest re-main-ing To spir-its of the blest.

On thee, the high and low-ly, Bend-ing be-fore the throne, Sing,
On thee our Lord vic-to-rious The Spir-it sent from Heav'n; And
Where gos-pel light is glow-ing With pure and ra-diant beams, And
To Ho-ly Ghost be prais-es, To Fa-ther and to Son; The

Ho-ly, Ho-ly, Ho-ly, To the great Three in One.
thus on thee most glo-rious A tri-ple light was given.
liv-ing wa-ter flow-ing With soul-re-fresh-ing streams.
Church her voice up-rais-es To Thee, blest Three in One. A-MEN.

Jesus, Lover of My Soul

Charles Wesley.

USED BY PERMISSION OF THE ESTATE
OF HAMILTON S. GORDON.

H. P. Danks.

1. Je - sus, Lov-er of my soul,   Let me to Thy bos-om fly,
2. Oth - er ref-uge have I none;   Hangs my help-less soul on Thee;
3. Thou, O Christ, art all I want;   More than all in Thee I find;
4. Plenteous grace with Thee is found,   Grace to cov-er all my sin;

While the near-er wa-ters roll,   While the tem-pest still is high.
Leave, oh, leave me not a - lone,   Still sup-port and com-fort me.
Raise the fall-en, cheer the faint,   Heal the sick, and lead the blind.
Let the heal-ing streams a - bound;   Make and keep me pure with-in.

Hide me, O, my Sav-ior, hide,   Till the storm of life is past;
All my trust on Thee is stayed,   All my help from Thee I bring;
Just and ho - ly is Thy name,   I am all un-right-eous-ness;
Thou of life the Foun-tain art,   Free - ly let me take of Thee;

Safe in - to the ha-ven guide,   O re-ceive my soul at last!
Cov - er my de-fense-less head   With the shad-ow of Thy wing.
Vile and full of sin I am,   Thou art full of truth and grace.
Spring Thou up within my heart,   Rise to all e - ter - ni - ty.   A-MEN.

Rock of Ages

Augustus M. Toplady.　　*Toplady. 7s. 6l.*　　Thomas Hastings.

1. Rock of A - ges, cleft for me, Let me hide my - self in Thee;
2. Could my tears for - ev - er flow, Could my zeal no lan-guor know,
3. While I draw this fleet-ing breath, When my eyes shall close in death,

Let the wa - ter and the blood, From Thy wound - ed side which flowed,
These for sin could not a - tone; Thou must save, and Thou a - lone:
When I rise to worlds un-known, And be - hold Thee on Thy throne,

Be of sin the doub - le cure, Save from wrath and make me pure.
In my hand no price I bring, Sim - ply to Thy cross I cling.
Rock of A - ges, cleft for me, Let me hide my - self in Thee. A - MEN.

[Second Tune.]　　*Martyn. 7s. D.*　　Simeon B. Marsh.
FINE.

1. { Je - sus, Lov - er of my soul, Let me to Thy bos - om fly, }
   { While the near - er wa - ters roll, While the tem-pest still is high! }
D. C.—Safe in - to the ha - ven guide, O re - ceive my soul at last.

D.C.

Hide me, O my Sav - ior, hide, Till the storm of life is past; A - MEN.

The Morning Light is Breaking

S. F. Smith.   Webb. 7s. 6s. D.   G. J. Webb.

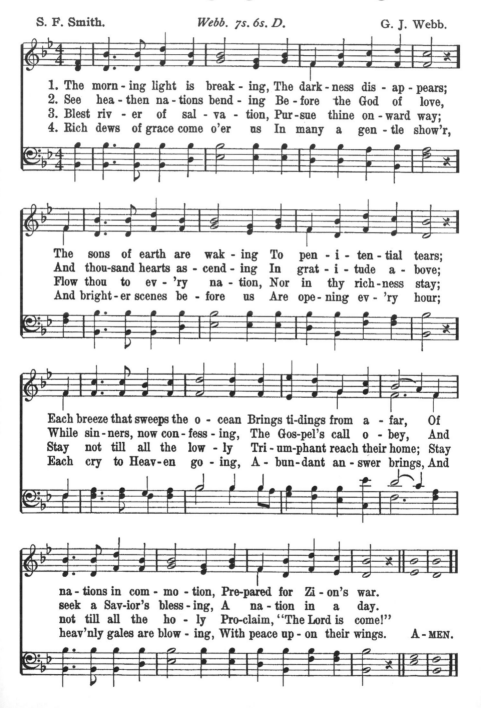

1. The morn-ing light is break-ing, The dark-ness dis-ap-pears;
2. See hea-then na-tions bend-ing Be-fore the God of love,
3. Blest riv-er of sal-va-tion, Pur-sue thine on-ward way;
4. Rich dews of grace come o'er us In many a gen-tle show'r,

The sons of earth are wak-ing To pen-i-ten-tial tears;
And thou-sand hearts as-cend-ing In grat-i-tude a-bove;
Flow thou to ev-'ry na-tion, Nor in thy rich-ness stay;
And bright-er scenes be-fore us Are ope-ning ev-'ry hour;

Each breeze that sweeps the o-cean Brings ti-dings from a-far, Of
While sin-ners, now con-fess-ing, The Gos-pel's call o-bey, And
Stay not till all the low-ly Tri-um-phant reach their home; Stay
Each cry to Heav-en go-ing, A-bun-dant an-swer brings, And

na-tions in com-mo-tion, Pre-pared for Zi-on's war.
seek a Sav-ior's bless-ing, A na-tion in a day.
not till all the ho-ly Pro-claim, "The Lord is come!"
heav'nly gales are blow-ing, With peace up-on their wings. A-MEN.

Stand Up for Jesus

G. Duffield. COPYRIGHT, 1917, BY E. O. EXCELL. E. O. Excell.

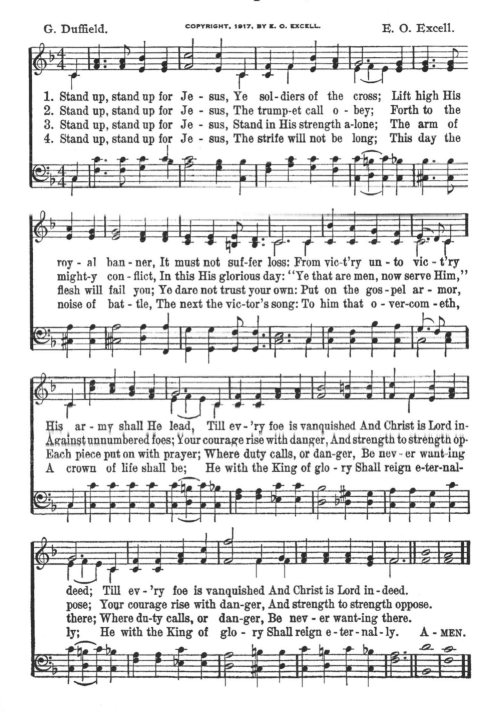

1. Stand up, stand up for Je - sus, Ye sol - diers of the cross; Lift high His
2. Stand up, stand up for Je - sus, The trump - et call o - bey; Forth to the
3. Stand up, stand up for Je - sus, Stand in His strength a - lone; The arm of
4. Stand up, stand up for Je - sus, The strife will not be long; This day the

roy - al ban - ner, It must not suf - fer loss: From vic-t'ry un - to vic - t'ry
might - y con - flict, In this His glorious day: "Ye that are men, now serve Him,"
flesh will fail you; Ye dare not trust your own: Put on the gos - pel ar - mor,
noise of bat - tle, The next the vic-tor's song: To him that o - ver-com - eth,

His ar - my shall He lead, Till ev - 'ry foe is vanquished And Christ is Lord in -
Against unnumbered foes; Your courage rise with danger, And strength to strength op -
Each piece put on with prayer; Where duty calls, or dan - ger, Be nev - er want-ing
A crown of life shall be; He with the King of glo - ry Shall reign e-ter-nal -

deed; Till ev - 'ry foe is vanquished And Christ is Lord in - deed.
pose; Your courage rise with dan - ger, And strength to strength oppose.
there; Where du-ty calls, or dan - ger, Be nev - er want-ing there.
ly; He with the King of glo - ry Shall reign e - ter - nal - ly. A - MEN.

It Came Upon the Midnight

Edmund H. Sears.   *Carol. C. M. D.*   Richard S. Willis.

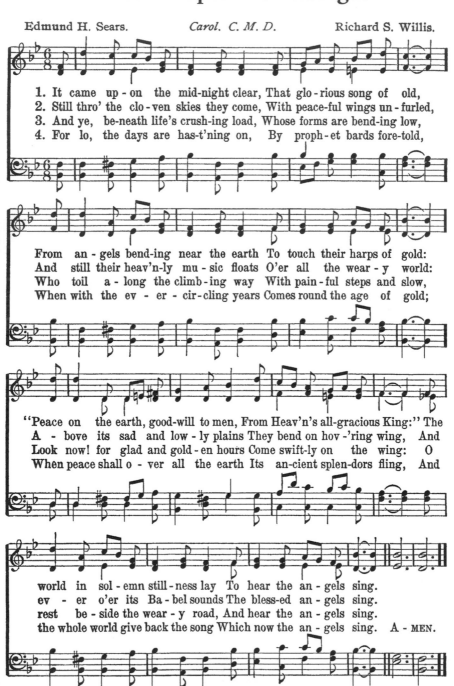

1. It came up-on the mid-night clear, That glo-rious song of old,
2. Still thro' the clo-ven skies they come, With peace-ful wings un-furled,
3. And ye, be-neath life's crush-ing load, Whose forms are bend-ing low,
4. For lo, the days are has-t'ning on, By proph-et bards fore-told,

From an-gels bend-ing near the earth To touch their harps of gold:
And still their heav'n-ly mu-sic floats O'er all the wear-y world:
Who toil a-long the climb-ing way With pain-ful steps and slow,
When with the ev-er-cir-cling years Comes round the age of gold;

"Peace on the earth, good-will to men, From Heav'n's all-gracious King:" The
A-bove its sad and low-ly plains They bend on hov-'ring wing, And
Look now! for glad and gold-en hours Come swift-ly on the wing: O
When peace shall o-ver all the earth Its an-cient splen-dors fling, And

world in sol-emn still-ness lay To hear the an-gels sing.
ev-er o'er its Ba-bel sounds The bless-ed an-gels sing.
rest be-side the wear-y road, And hear the an-gels sing.
the whole world give back the song Which now the an-gels sing. A-MEN.

Crown Him with Many Crowns

Matthew Bridges.   *Diademata. S. M. D.*   George J. Elvey.

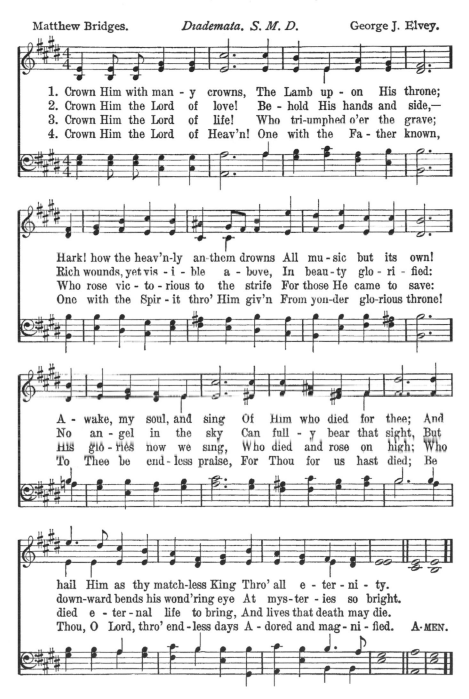

1. Crown Him with man - y crowns, The Lamb up - on His throne;
2. Crown Him the Lord of love! Be - hold His hands and side,—
3. Crown Him the Lord of life! Who tri-umphed o'er the grave;
4. Crown Him the Lord of Heav'n! One with the Fa - ther known,

Hark! how the heav'n-ly an-them drowns All mu - sic but its own!
Rich wounds, yet vis - i - ble a - bove, In beau - ty glo - ri - fied:
Who rose vic - to - rious to the strife For those He came to save:
One with the Spir - it thro' Him giv'n From yon-der glo-rious throne!

A - wake, my soul, and sing Of Him who died for thee; And
No an - gel in the sky Can full - y bear that sight, But
His glo - ries now we sing, Who died and rose on high; Who
To Thee be end - less praise, For Thou for us hast died; Be

hail Him as thy match-less King Thro' all e - ter - ni - ty.
down-ward bends his wond'ring eye At mys-ter - ies so bright.
died e - ter - nal life to bring, And lives that death may die.
Thou, O Lord, thro' end - less days A - dored and mag - ni - fied. A-MEN.

The Church's One Foundation

Samuel J. Stone.   *Aurelia. 7s. 6s. D.*   Samuel S. Wesley.

1. The Church-'s one foun - da - tion Is Je - sus Christ her Lord;
2. E - lect from ev - 'ry na - tion, Yet one o'er all the earth,
3. 'Mid toil and trib - u - la - tion, And tu - mult of her war,
4. Yet she on earth hath un - ion With God the Three in One,

She is His new cre - a - tion By wa - ter and the word:
Her char - ter of sal - va - tion, One Lord, one faith, one birth;
She waits the con - sum - ma - tion Of peace for - ev - er - more;
And mys - tic sweet com - mun - ion With those whose rest is won:

From Heav'n He came and sought her To be His ho - ly bride; With
One ho - ly name she bless - es, Par - takes one ho - ly food, And
Till, with the vi - sion glo - rious, Her long - ing eyes are blest, And
O hap - py ones and ho - ly! Lord, give us grace that we, Like

His own blood He bought her, And for her life He died.
to one hope she press - es, With ev - 'ry grace en - dued.
the great church vic - to - rious Shall be the church at rest.
them, the meek and low - ly, On high may dwell with Thee. A-MEN.

Joy to the World

Isaac Watts. *Antioch. C. M.* George F. Handel.

1. Joy to the world! the Lord is come; Let earth receive her King; Let ev-'ry heart pre-pare Him room, And Heav'n and na-ture sing, And Heav'n and na-ture sing, And Heav'n, and Heav'n and na-ture sing.

2. Joy to the earth! the Sav-ior reigns; Let men their songs em-ploy; While fields and floods, rocks, hills and plains Re-peat the sound-ing joy, Re-peat the sound-ing joy, Re-peat, re-peat the sound-ing joy.

3. No more let sins and sor-rows grow, Nor thorns in-fest the ground; He comes to make His bless-ings flow Far as the curse is found, Far as the curse is found, Far as, far as the curse is found.

4. He rules the world with truth and grace, And makes the na-tions prove The glo-ries of His right-eous-ness, And won-ders of His love, And won-ders of His love, And won-ders, and won-ders of His love. A-MEN.

The Son of God Goes Forth to War

Reginald Heber.   *All Saints New. C. M. D.*   Henry S. Cutler.

1. The Son of God goes forth to war, A king-ly crown to gain;
2. The mar-tyr first, whose ea-gle eye Could pierce be-yond the grave,
3. A glo-rious band, the cho-sen few On whom the Spir-it came,
4. A no-ble ar-my, men and boys, The ma-tron and the maid,

His blood-red ban-ner streams a-far: Who fol-lows in His train?
Who saw his Mas-ter in the sky, And called on Him to save:
Twelve valiant saints, their hope they knew, And mocked the cross and flame:
A-round the Sav-ior's throne re-joice, In robes of light ar-rayed:

Who best can drink his cup of woe, Tri-um-phant o-ver pain, Who
Like Him, with par-don on His tongue In midst of mor-tal pain, He
They met the tyrant's brandished steel, The li-on's go-ry mane; They
They climbed the steep as-cent of Heav'n Thro' per-il, toil, and pain: O

pa-tient bears his cross be-low, He fol-lows in His train.
prayed for them that did the wrong: Who fol-lows in His train?
bowed their necks the death to feel: Who fol-lows in their train?
God, to us may grace be given To fol-low in their train. A-MEN.

Onward, Christian Soldiers

Sabine Baring-Gould.   *St. Gertrude. 6s. 5s D.*   Arthur Sullivan.

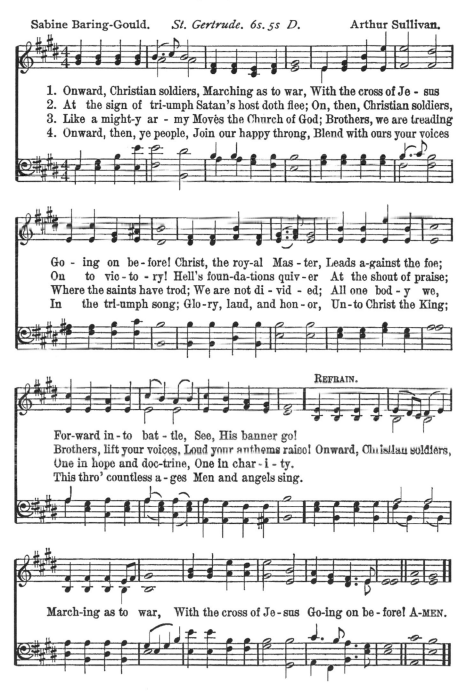

1. Onward, Christian soldiers, Marching as to war, With the cross of Je - sus
2. At the sign of tri-umph Satan's host doth flee; On, then, Christian soldiers,
3. Like a might-y ar - my Moves the Church of God; Brothers, we are treading
4. Onward, then, ye people, Join our happy throng, Blend with ours your voices

Go - ing on be - fore! Christ, the roy-al Mas - ter, Leads a-gainst the foe;
On to vic - to - ry! Hell's foun-da-tions quiv - er At the shout of praise;
Where the saints have trod; We are not di - vid - ed; All one bod - y we,
In the tri-umph song; Glo-ry, laud, and hon - or, Un-to Christ the King;

REFRAIN.

For-ward in - to bat - tle, See, His banner go!
Brothers, lift your voices, Loud your anthems raise! Onward, Christian soldiers,
One in hope and doc-trine, One in char - i - ty.
This thro' countless a - ges Men and angels sing.

March-ing as to war, With the cross of Je - sus Go-ing on be - fore! A-MEN.

It Is Well With My Soul

H. G. Spafford.

P. P. Bliss.

1. When peace, like a riv-er, at-tend-eth my way, When sor-rows like
2. Though Sa-tan should buf-fet, tho' tri-als should come, Let this blest as-
3. My sin— oh, the bliss of this glo-ri-ous tho't—My sin—not in
4. And, Lord, haste the day when the faith shall be sight, The clouds be rolled

sea-bil-lows roll; What-ev-er my lot, Thou hast taught me to say,
sur-ance con-trol, That Christ has re-gard-ed my help-less es-tate,
part, but the whole, Is nailed to the cross and I bear it no more,
back as a scroll, The trump shall resound and the Lord shall de-scend,

Chorus.

It is well, it is well with my soul.
And hath shed His own blood for my soul. It is well . . . . with my
Praise the Lord, praise the Lord, O my soul!
"E-ven so"—it is well with my soul. It is well

soul, ... It is well, it is well with my soul. A-MEN.
with my soul,

The Comforter Has Come

F. Bottome.

Wm. J. Kirkpatrick.

1. O spread the ti-dings 'round, wher-ev-er man is found, Wher-
2. The long, long night is past, the morn-ing breaks at last, And
3. Lo, the great King of kings, with heal-ing in His wings, To
4. O bound-less love di-vine! how shall this tongue of mine To

ev-er hu-man hearts and hu-man woes a-bound; Let ev-'ry Chris-tian
hushed the dreadful wail and fu-ry of the blast, As o'er the gold-en
ev-'ry cap-tive soul a full de-liv-'rance brings; And thro' the va-cant
wond'ring mor-tals tell the match-less grace di-vine—That I, a child of

D.S.—Ho-ly Ghost from Heav'n, The Fa-ther's prom-ise giv'n; O spread the ti-dings

tongue pro-claim the joy-ful sound: The Com-fort-er has come!
hills the day ad-vanc-es fast! The Com-fort-er has come!
cells the song of tri-umph rings; The Com-fort-er has come!
hell, should in His im-age shine! The Com-fort-er has come!

'round, wher-ev-er man is found—The Com-fort-er has come!

CHORUS.

The Com-fort-er has come, The Com-fort-er has come! The A-MEN.

D. S.

The Church in the Wildwood

W. S. P.   NEW ARRANGEMENT OF WORDS AND MUSIC COPYRIGHT, 1910, BY E. O. EXCELL.   Dr. Wm. S. Pitts.

1. There's a church in the val-ley by the wild-wood, No love-li-er spot in the dale; No place is so dear to my child-hood As the lit-tle brown church in the vale.

2. Oh, come to the church in the wild-wood, To the trees where the wild flow-ers bloom; Where the part-ing hymn will be chant-ed, We will weep by the side of the tomb.

3. How sweet on a clear, Sab-bath morn-ing, To list to the clear ring-ing bell; Its tones so sweet-ly are call-ing, Oh, come to the church in the vale.

4. From the church in the val-ley by the wild-wood, When day fades a-way in-to night, I would fain from this spot of my child-hood Wing my way to the man-sions of light.

D. S.—No spot is so dear to my child-hood As the little brown church in the vale.

FINE. CHORUS.

Come to the church in the wild - wood, Oh, come to the church in the vale; A-MEN.

Oh, come;

D. S.

Stepping in the Light

L. H. Edmunds.

Wm. J. Kirkpatrick.

1. Try - ing to walk in the steps of the Sav - ior, Try - ing to fol - low our
2. Pressing more closely to Him who is lead - ing, When we are tempted to
3. Walking in foot-steps of gen - tle for-bear-ance, Footsteps of faith-ful-ness,
4. Try - ing to walk in the steps of the Sav - ior, Up - ward, still up - ward we'll

Sav - ior and King; Shap - ing our lives by His bless - ed ex - am - ple,
turn from the way; Trust - ing the arm that is strong to de - fend us,
mer - cy, and love, Look - ing to Him for the grace free - ly prom-ised,
fol - low our Guide; When we shall see Him, "the King in His beau - ty,"

CHORUS.

Hap-py, how hap-py, the songs that we bring.
Hap-py, how hap-py, our prais-es each day. How beau-ti - ful to walk in the
Hap-py, how hap-py, our jour-ney a - bove.
Hap-py, how hap-py, our place at His side.

steps of the Sav - ior, Stepping in the light, Step-ping in the light; How

beau-ti-ful to walk in the steps of the Sav-ior, Led in paths of light. A-MEN.

No One Loves You So

Rev. Alfred Barratt.   COPYRIGHT, 1919, BY E. O. EXCELL.   Henry P. Morton.
                              WORDS AND MUSIC.

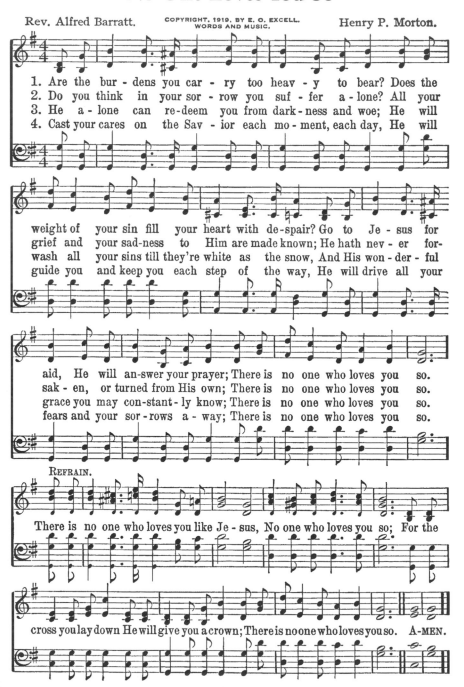

1. Are the bur - dens you car - ry too heav - y to bear? Does the
2. Do you think in your sor - row you suf - fer a - lone? All your
3. He a - lone can re - deem you from dark - ness and woe; He will
4. Cast your cares on the Sav - ior each mo - ment, each day, He will

weight of your sin fill your heart with de-spair? Go to Je - sus for
grief and your sad-ness to Him are made known; He hath nev - er for-
wash all your sins till they're white as the snow, And His won - der - ful
guide you and keep you each step of the way, He will drive all your

aid, He will an-swer your prayer; There is no one who loves you so.
sak - en, or turned from His own; There is no one who loves you so.
grace you may con-stant - ly know; There is no one who loves you so.
fears and your sor - rows a - way; There is no one who loves you so.

REFRAIN.

There is no one who loves you like Je - sus, No one who loves you so; For the

cross you lay down He will give you a crown; There is no one who loves you so. A-MEN.

Happy in Jesus

Fanny J. Crosby.

Wm. J. Kirkpatrick.

1. Hap-py in Je-sus, hap-py in Je-sus, I will de-clare it a-broad;
2. Cling-ing to Je-sus, on-ly to Je-sus, O what a com-fort is mine;
3. Walking with Je-sus, on-ly with Je-sus, Sweet-ly I jour-ney a-long;

CHO.—Hap-py in Je-sus, hap-py in Je-sus, I will de-clare it a-broad;

Thro' His a-tone-ment, precious a-tone-ment, I have found fa-vor with God.
I will a-dore Him, yes, I will praise Him, Je-sus, my Sav-ior di-vine.
I have believed Him, I have re-ceived Him, He is my joy and my song.

Thro' His a-tone-ment, pre-cious a-tone-ment, I have found fa-vor with God.

Kind-ly He sought me, ten-der-ly bro't me Out of the des-ert so wild;
Un-der His watch-care peace-ful-ly hid-ing, Faith my Re-deem-er can see;
Watching me ev-er, leav-ing me nev-er, Still my Pro-tect-or is nigh;

Now I can trust Him, thankfully trust Him, Since He has made me His child.
An-gels in glo-ry, tell-ing the sto-ry, Now are rejoicing with me.
Saved by His mer-cy, in-fi-nite mer-cy, Who is so hap-py as I? .. A-MEN.

My Mother's Bible

M. B. Williams. COPYRIGHT, 1893, BY CHARLIE D. TILLMAN. Charlie D. Tillman.

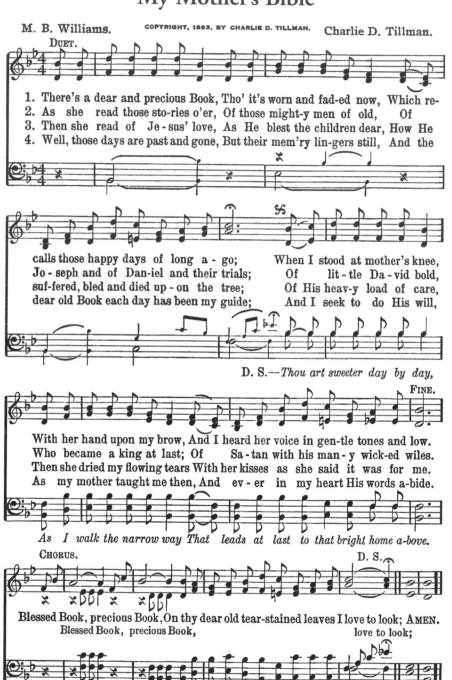

DUET.

1. There's a dear and precious Book, Tho' it's worn and fad-ed now, Which re-
2. As she read those sto-ries o'er, Of those might-y men of old, Of
3. Then she read of Je-sus' love, As He blest the children dear, How He
4. Well, those days are past and gone, But their mem'ry lin-gers still, And the

calls those happy days of long a-go; When I stood at mother's knee,
Jo-seph and of Dan-iel and their trials; Of lit-tle Da-vid bold,
suf-fered, bled and died up-on the tree; Of His heav-y load of care,
dear old Book each day has been my guide; And I seek to do His will,

D. S.—*Thou art sweeter day by day,*

FINE.

With her hand upon my brow, And I heard her voice in gen-tle tones and low.
Who became a king at last; Of Sa-tan with his man-y wick-ed wiles.
Then she dried my flowing tears With her kisses as she said it was for me.
As my mother taught me then, And ev-er in my heart His words a-bide.

As I walk the narrow way That leads at last to that bright home a-bove.

CHORUS. D. S.

Blessed Book, precious Book, On thy dear old tear-stained leaves I love to look; AMEN.
Blessed Book, precious Book, love to look;

I Am Thine, O Lord

Fanny J. Crosby.

W. H. Doane.

1. I am Thine, O Lord, I have heard Thy voice, And it told Thy
2. Con-se-crate me now to Thy serv-ice, Lord, By the pow'r of
3. O the pure de-light of a sin-gle hour That be-fore Thy
4. There are depths of love that I can-not know Till I cross the

love to me; But I long to rise in the arms of faith, And be
grace di-vine; Let my soul look up with a stead-fast hope, And my
throne I spend, When I kneel in prayer, and with Thee, my God, I com-
nar-row sea; There are heights of joy that I may not reach Till I

REFRAIN.

clo-ser drawn to Thee.
will be lost in Thine. Draw me near - - er, near-er, bless-ed
mune as friend with friend!
rest in peace with Thee. near - er, near-er,

Lord, To the cross where Thou hast died; Draw me near-er, near-er,

near-er, bless-ed Lord, To Thy pre-cious, bleed-ing side. A-MEN.

I Must Tell Jesus

E. A. H.   COPYRIGHT, 1893, BY THE HOFFMAN MUSIC CO.   Rev. E. A. Hoffman.

1. I must tell Je - sus all of my tri - als; I can-not bear these
2. I must tell Je - sus all of my troub-les; He is a kind, com-
3. Tempted and tried I need a great Sav - ior, One who can help my
4. O how the world to e - vil al - lures me! O how my heart is

bur - dens a - lone; In my dis - tress He kind - ly will help me;
pas - sion-ate Friend; If I but ask Him, He will de - liv - er,
bur - dens to bear; I must tell Je - sus, I must tell Je - sus;
tempt-ed to sin! I must tell Je - sus, and He will help me

CHORUS.

He ev - er loves and cares for His own. I must tell Je - sus!
Make of my troub-les quick - ly an end.
He all my cares and sor - rows will share.
O - ver the world the vic - t'ry to win.

I must tell Je - sus! I can-not bear my bur-dens a - lone; I must tell

Je - sus! I must tell Je-sus! Je-sus can help me, Je-sus a - lone.   A - MEN.

The Spacious Firmament

Joseph Addison. *Creation. L. M. D.* Francis Joseph Haydn.

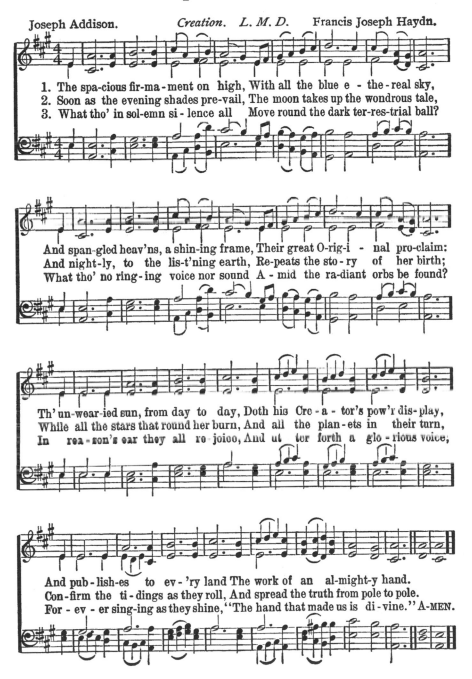

1. The spa-cious fir-ma-ment on high, With all the blue e - the-real sky,
2. Soon as the evening shades pre-vail, The moon takes up the wondrous tale,
3. What tho' in sol-emn si - lence all Move round the dark ter-res-trial ball?

And span-gled heav'ns, a shin-ing frame, Their great O-rig-i - nal pro-claim:
And night-ly, to the lis-t'ning earth, Re-peats the sto-ry of her birth;
What tho' no ring-ing voice nor sound A - mid the ra-diant orbs be found?

Th' un-wear-ied sun, from day to day, Doth his Cre - a - tor's pow'r dis-play,
While all the stars that round her burn, And all the plan-ets in their turn,
In rea-son's ear they all re-joice, And ut - ter forth a glo - rious voice;

And pub-lish-es to ev-'ry land The work of an al-might-y hand.
Con-firm the ti - dings as they roll, And spread the truth from pole to pole.
For - ev - er sing-ing as they shine, "The hand that made us is di - vine." A-MEN.

Safe In His Keeping

E. E. Hewitt.

Henry P. Morton.

1. Safe in the keep-ing of Je - sus my King, Kept by His won-der-ful pow'r; Good-ness and mer - cy I grate-ful-ly sing, Look-ing to Him ev - 'ry hour.
2. Held by the hand that is might-y to save, Faith lifts a song in the storm; Walk-ing with Him o - ver life's storm-y wave, He will His prom-ise per - form.
3. Safe in the keep-ing of Je - sus my Lord, On His strong arm will I rest; New gifts of love ev-'ry day will re - cord, Do - ing His will I am blest.

CHORUS.

Safe in His keep-ing, wak-ing or sleep-ing, O, may I dai - ly serve Him whom I love; Filled with the Spir - it, kept by His grace, Till I shall see Him and praise Him a - bove. A-MEN.

My Heart Keeps Right

Lizzie DeArmond.

B. D. Ackley.

1. There's a song of joy, I sing it ev-'ry day, For my ev-'ry sin the
2. As I live for Him each burden seems so light; While He walks with me my
3. All my doubts are past, I am se-cure at last; Tho' my strength may fail, my

Lord has washed a-way; Trust-ing in His word, I yield to His con-trol,
heart is keep-ing right; In the nar-row way I'm press-ing tow'rd the goal,
an-chor hold-eth fast; Tho' I once was lost, His grace hath made me whole,

CHORUS.

Since the lov-ing Je-sus saved my soul. . . . . . My heart keeps right since
Since Je-sus saved my soul.

Je-sus saved my soul; My ev'ry tho't is under His control; With songs of joy I'm

pressing tow'rd the goal; My heart keeps right since Jesus saved my soul. A-MEN.

O That Will Be Glory

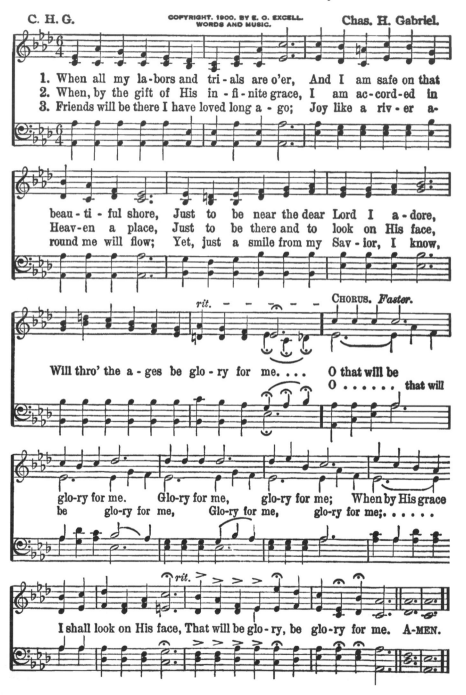

C. H. G.

COPYRIGHT, 1900, BY E. O. EXCELL.
WORDS AND MUSIC.

Chas. H. Gabriel.

1. When all my la-bors and tri-als are o'er, And I am safe on that
2. When, by the gift of His in-fi-nite grace, I am ac-cord-ed in
3. Friends will be there I have loved long a-go; Joy like a riv-er a-

beau-ti-ful shore, Just to be near the dear Lord I a-dore,
Heav-en a place, Just to be there and to look on His face,
round me will flow; Yet, just a smile from my Sav-ior, I know,

Will thro' the a-ges be glo-ry for me. ....   O that will be
                                                O ...... that will

glo-ry for me.   Glo-ry for me,   glo-ry for me;   When by His grace
be   glo-ry for me,   Glo-ry for me,   glo-ry for me; ......

I shall look on His face, That will be glo-ry, be glo-ry for me.   A-MEN.

The Way of the Cross Leads Home

Jessie Brown Pounds.   COPYRIGHT, 1906, BY CHAS. H. GABRIEL.   Chas. H. Gabriel.
COPYRIGHT, 1907, BY E. O. EXCELL.

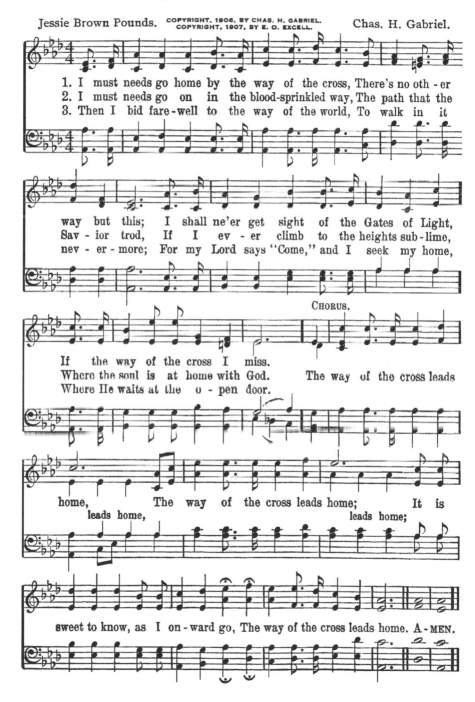

1. I must needs go home by the way of the cross, There's no oth-er
2. I must needs go on in the blood-sprinkled way, The path that the
3. Then I bid fare-well to the way of the world, To walk in it

way but this; I shall ne'er get sight of the Gates of Light,
Sav-ior trod, If I ev-er climb to the heights sub-lime,
nev-er-more; For my Lord says "Come," and I seek my home,

If the way of the cross I miss.
Where the soul is at home with God.
Where He waits at the o-pen door.

CHORUS.

The way of the cross leads home, The way of the cross leads home; It is
leads home,   leads home;

sweet to know, as I on-ward go, The way of the cross leads home. A-MEN.

Abundantly Able to Save

Elisha A. Hoffman.   COPYRIGHT, 1884, BY HE BIGLOW & MAIN CO.   Philip P. Bliss.
                           USED BY PERMISSION.

1. Who-ev-er re - ceiv - eth the Cru-ci - fied One, Who-ev-er be - liev - eth on
2. Who-ev-er re - ceiv - eth the message of God, And trusts in the power of the
3. Who-ev-er re - pents and forsakes ev-'ry sin, And o-pens his heart for the

God's on - ly Son,   A free and a   per - fect sal-va-tion shall have:
soul-cleans-ing blood, A full and e - ter - nal re-demp-tion shall have:
Lord to come in,   A pres-ent and per - fect sal-va-tion shall have:

FINE. CHORUS.

For He is a - bun-dant-ly a - ble to save. My brother, the Mas - ter is
D.S.—And He is a - bun-dant-ly a - ble to save.   Brother, the Mas-ter is

call-ing for thee; .. His grace and His mer - cy are wondrously free; ..
come, and is call-ing for thee;   Brother, His grace and His mercy are wondrously free;

D.S.

His blood as a ran - - som for sin-ners He gave, ...   A - MEN.
Broth-er, His blood as a ran-som for sin-ners He gave,

Sweeter As the Days Go By

James Rowe.

Hamp Sewell.

1. O the love of Je-sus means so much to me, Keeps my path-way shin-ing,
2. Precious, lov-ing Sav-ior, all a-long the way, Words of cheer and com-fort
3. He, I know, will keep me, He will hold me fast Till my earth-ly tri-als

keeps me pure and free; More and more I praise Him, for He seems to be
I have heard Him say, And He grows more pre-cious to my soul each day,
be for-ev-er past; He will be, un-til I see His face at last,

Chorus.

Sweet-er as the days go by. Sweet-er as the days go by, ...
as the days go by,

Sweet-er as the mo-ments fly; . . . . . . Sweet-er and the dear-er
as the mo-ments fly;

as to me He draw-eth near-er, Sweet-er as the days go by. A-MEN.

Grace Sufficient

W. S. M.

W. S. Martin.

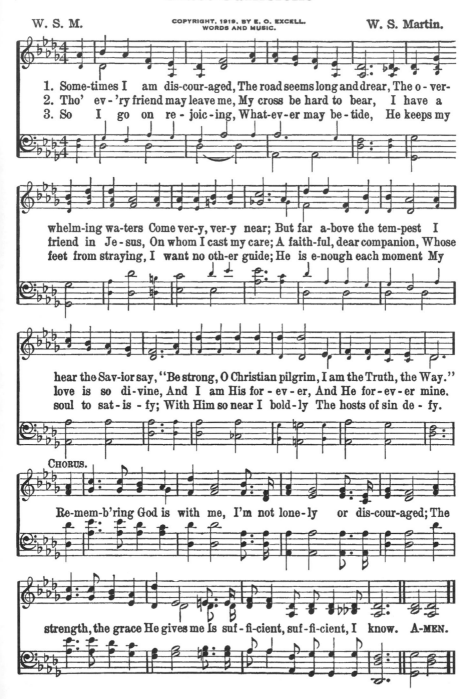

1. Some-times I am dis-cour-aged, The road seems long and drear, The o - ver-
2. Tho' ev - 'ry friend may leave me, My cross be hard to bear, I have a
3. So I go on re - joic-ing, What-ev-er may be-tide, He keeps my

whelm-ing wa-ters Come ver-y, ver-y near; But far a-bove the tem-pest I
friend in Je - sus, On whom I cast my care; A faith-ful, dear companion, Whose
feet from straying, I want no oth-er guide; He is e-nough each moment My

hear the Sav-ior say, "Be strong, O Christian pilgrim, I am the Truth, the Way."
love is so di-vine, And I am His for - ev - er, And He for-ev-er mine.
soul to sat-is - fy; With Him so near I bold-ly The hosts of sin de - fy.

CHORUS.

Re-mem-b'ring God is with me, I'm not lone-ly or dis-cour-aged; The

strength, the grace He gives me Is suf - fi-cient, suf-fi-cient, I know. A-MEN.

The King's Business

Dr. E. T. Cassel.
Flora H. Cassel.

1. I am a stranger here, with-in a foreign land; My home is far a-way, up-on a gold-en strand; Am-bas-sa-dor to be of realms be-yond the sea,

2. This is the King's command: that all men, ev'rywhere, Repent and turn a-way from sin's seductive snare; That all who will o-bey, with Him shall reign for aye,

3. My home is bright-er far than Sharon's ro-sy plain, E-ter-nal life and joy thro'-out its vast domain; My Sov'reign bids me tell how mortals there may dwell,

CHORUS.

I'm here on business for my King.
And that's my business for my King. This is the mes-sage that I
And that's my business for my King.

bring, A mes-sage an-gels fain would sing: "Oh, be ye rec-on-ciled,"
Thus saith my Lord and King, "Oh, be ye rec-on-ciled to God." A-MEN.

I Will Not Forget Thee

C. H. G.

COPYRIGHT, 1889, BY E. O. EXCELL.
WORDS AND MUSIC.

Chas. H. Gabriel.

1. Sweet is the prom-ise—"I will not for-get thee," Nothing can mo-lest or
2. Trusting the prom-ise—"I will not for-get thee," Onward will I go with
3. When at the gold-en por-tals I am stand-ing, All my trib-u-la-tions,

turn my soul a-way; E'en tho' the night be dark with-in the val-ley,
songs of joy and love; Tho' earth de-spise me, tho' my friends for-sake me.
all my sor-rows past, How sweet to hear the bless-ed proc-la-ma-tion,

CHORUS.

Just be-yond is shin-ing one e-ter-nal day. I . . . . . will not forget thee or
I shall be re-mem-bered in my home a-bove.
"En-ter, faithful servant, welcome home at last!" I will not for-get thee, I will nev-er

leave thee; In my hands I'll hold thee, in my arms I'll fold thee; I . . . . . will
leave thee;   I will not for-get

rit. . . . . . .

not for-get thee or leave thee; I am thy Re-deem-er, I will care for thee. A-MEN.
thee, for-get

The Kingdom Coming

Mrs. M. B. C. Slade.   R. M. McIntosh.

1. From all the dark pla - ces Of earth's hea-then ra - ces, O see how the
2. The sun-light is glanc-ing O'er ar - mies ad-vanc-ing, To con-quer the
3. With shout-ing and sing-ing, And ju - bi - lant ring-ing, Their arms of re-

thick shad-ows fly! The voice of sal - va - tion A-wakes ev - 'ry na - tion,
king-doms of sin; Our Lord shall pos-sess them, His presence shall bless them,
bel - lion cast down, At last ev - 'ry na - tion The Lord of sal - va - tion,

CHORUS.

Come o - ver and help us, they cry.
His beau - ty shall en - ter them in.   The king - dom is com - ing, O
Their King and Re-deem - er shall crown!

tell ye the sto - ry, God's ban-ner ex - alt - ed shall be! The earth shall be

full of His knowledge and glo-ry, As wa-ters that cov-er the sea.   A - MEN.

Jesus Is Leading Me

Be of Good Courage Today

Rev. Alfred Barratt.

Wm. J. Kirkpatrick.

1. Be of good courage, be brave, and be strong; When the pathway is drear-y and
2. Be of good cour-age for He is your Stay, And will keep you in safe-ty while
3. Be of good cour-age what-ev-er be-tide, For the Sav-ior has promised His

dark-some, and long, Noth-ing can harm you what-ev-er be-tide, While the
trav-'ling life's way, Won-der-ful mer-cy and grace to im-part; He will
chil-dren to guide; Dan-gers may threaten you, be not dis-mayed, "I will

Sav-ior is with you as Lead-er and Guide.
com-fort, il-lu-mine, and strengthen your heart. Be of good cour-age, good
nev-er for-sake you," the Sav-ior hath said.

CHORUS.

cour-age to-day, Be of good courage, good courage to-day, What-ev-er be-
day, to-day, to-day, to-day,

ritard. - - -

tide, In love He will guide—Oh, be of good courage, good courage to-day. A-MEN.

Will There Be Any Stars?

E. E. Hewitt

Jno. R. Sweney.

1. I am think-ing to-day of that beau-ti-ful land I shall reach when the
2. In the strength of the Lord let me la-bor and pray, Let me watch as a
3. Oh, what joy it will be when His face I be-hold, Liv-ing gems at His

sun go-eth down; When thro' wonderful grace by my Sav-ior I stand, Will there
win-ner of souls; That bright stars may be mine in the glo-ri-ous day, When His
feet to lay down; It would sweeten my bliss in the cit-y of gold, Should there

Chorus.

be an-y stars in my crown?
praise like the sea-bil-low rolls. Will there be an-y stars, an-y stars in my
be an-y stars in my crown.

crown When at evening the sun go-eth down? . . . When I wake with the blest
go-eth down?

In the mansions of rest, Will there be an-y stars in my crown? . . A-MEN.
an-y stars in my crown?

While the Years Are Rolling On

Harriet B. McKeever.

Jno. R. Sweney.

1. In a world so full of weep-ing, While the years are roll-ing on,
2. There's no time to waste in sigh-ing, While the years are roll-ing on;
3. Let us strengthen one an-oth-er, While the years are roll-ing on;
4. Friends we love are quick-ly fly-ing, While the years are roll-ing on;

Chris-tian souls the watch are keep-ing, While the years are roll-ing on.
Time is fly-ing, souls are dy-ing, While the years are roll-ing on.
Seek to raise a fall-en broth-er, While the years are roll-ing on.
No more part-ing, no more dy-ing, While the years are roll-ing on.

While our jour-ney we pur-sue, With the ha-ven still in view,
Lov-ing words a soul may win From the wretch-ed paths of sin;
This is work for ev-'ry hand, Till, thro'-out cre-a-tion's land,
In the world be-yond the tomb Sor-row nev-er-more can come,

There is work for us to do, While the years are roll-ing on.
We may bring the wan-d'rers in, While the years are roll-ing on.
Ar-mies for the Lord shall stand, While the years are roll-ing on.
When we meet in that blest home, While the years are roll-ing on.

D.S.—*O, the good we may be do-ing, While the years are roll-ing on.*

CHORUS.

Are roll-ing on,(Are roll-ing on,)Are roll-ing on,(Are roll-ing on,) A-MEN.

Victory Through Grace

Sallie Martin.   Jno. R. Sweney.

1. Con-quer-ing now and still to con-quer, Rid-eth a King in His might,
2. Con-quer-ing now and still to con-quer, Who is this won-der-ful King?
3. Con-quer-ing now and still to con-quer, Je-sus, Thou Ru-ler of all,

Lead-ing the host of all the faith-ful In-to the midst of the fight;
Whence are the ar-mies which He lead-eth, While of His glo-ry they sing?
Thrones and their scepters all shall per-ish, Crowns and their splendor shall fall,

See them with cour-age ad-vanc-ing, Clad in their bril-liant ar-ray,
He is our Lord and Re-deem-er, Sav-ior and Mon-arch di-vine;
Yet shall the ar-mies Thou lead-est, Faith-ful and true to the last,

Shout-ing the name of their Lead-er, Hear them ex-ult-ing-ly say:
They are the stars that for-ev-er Bright in His King-dom will shine.
Find in Thy man-sions e-ter-nal Rest, when their war-fare is past.

D. S.—*Yet to the true and the faith-ful Vic-t'ry is prom-ised thro' grace.*

CHORUS.   D.S.

Not to the strong is the bat-tle, Not to the swift is the race,   A-MEN.

In Heavenly Pastures

Mrs. A. M. Whitaker.   COPYRIGHT, 1919, BY THE JOHN CHURCH CO.   Geo. F. Root.

1. In the heav'n-ly pas-tures fair, 'Neath the ten - der Shep-herd's care,
2. Far from all the noise and strife That dis - turb our dai - ly life,
3. O how good and true and kind, Seek - ing His stray sheep to find,

Let us rest be - side the liv - ing stream to - day;
Let us pause a - while in si - lence and a - dore;
If they wan - der in - to dan - ger from His side;

Calm - ly there in peace re - cline, Drink-ing in the truth di - vine,
Then the sound of His dear voice Will our wait - ing souls re - joice,
Ev - er close - ly may we tread Where His ho - ly feet have led,

D. S.—Tho' re-vealed with-in the word Of our Shep-herd and our Lord,
FINE.

As His lov - ing call we now with joy o - bey. (joy o - bey.)
As He nam - eth us His own for - ev - er - more. (ev - er - more.)
So at last with Him in Heav'n we may a - bide. (may a - bide.)

By the pure in heart a - lone can they be seen. (ev - er seen.)
CHORUS.   D.S.

Glorious stream of life eternal, Beauteous fields of living green, (living green.) AMEN.

Thy Kingdom Come

Rev. C. McKibbin.

Chas. H. Gabriel.

1. Thy kingdom come! and shall not each one sing it, On land and sea, where'er His
2. Thy kingdom come! O haste to tell the message, The world is dy - ing for the
3. Thy kingdom come! He waits to bless the nations, 'Tis ours to bring them quickly

ban-ner goes? Thy kingdom come! shall we not strive to bring it, The grace that
word of God; Send out the light, that Christ may see the fruitage, The world re-
to His feet; Make this the time to tram-ple sin's foundations, And lead the

CHORUS.

saves the world from hu-man woes?
deemed that His own feet have trod. Thy kingdom come! the glo-rious tri-umph
er - ring to the mer-cy-seat.

hasten, When peoples all shall crown Him King of kings; . . . . . Saints shall re-
shall crown Him King of kings;

joice, and angels stop to listen, While earth His everlasting glo-ry sings. AMEN.

His Love Keeps Me Singing

James Rowe.

Hamp Sewell.

1. Oh, the love of Je-sus Bright-ens all my days, Keeps me sing-ing
2. Tho' the bur-den's heav-y, Foes as-sail in vain, With His love o'er-
3. Thus 'twill be in glo-ry, By the crys-tal sea; In com-mun-ion

all the time Hap-py songs of praise: Storms may beat a-bout me, Sky and
flow-ing me, Vic-tor I re-main: Thro' the toil of noon-day, Thro' the
with my Lord, Love my theme will be: More and more thro' a-ges, In that

path be dim, Still His love will keep me Sing-ing a song to Him.
mid-night long, Love di-vine will keep me Sing-ing to Him my song.
home a-bove, I will sing of Je-sus And His re-deem-ing love.

CHORUS.

His love keeps me sing-ing, ... His love makes me true; ....
sing-ing, makes me true;

The love of Je-sus keeps me sing-ing The whole day through. A-MEN.

Scatter Sunshine

Lanta Wilson Smith.

E. O. Excell.

1. In a world where sor - row Ev - er will be known, Where are found the
2. Slight-est ac - tions oft - en Meet the sor - est needs, For the world wants
3. When the days are gloom-y Sing some hap-py song; Meet the world's re-

need - y, And the sad and lone, How much joy and com - fort
dai - ly Lit - tle kind - ly deeds; Oh, what care and sor - row
pin - ing With a cour-age strong; Go with faith un-daunt-ed

You can all be - stow, If you scat - ter sun-shine Ev-'ry-where you go.
You may help re - move, With your songs and courage, Sym-pa-thy and love.
Thro' the ills of life; Scat-ter smiles and sunshine O'er its toil and strife.

CHORUS.

Scat - - ter sun-shine all a-long your way, . . . Cheer and bless and
Scat-ter the smiles and sun-shine all a-long, o - ver the way,

bright-en Ev-'ry pass-ing day; . . Ev-'ry pass-ing day. A - MEN.
pass - ing day;

Sound the Battle Cry

W. F. S.   Wm. F. Sherwin.

1. Sound the bat - tle cry! See, the foe is nigh; Raise the stand-ard high
2. Strong to meet the foe, March-ing on we go, While our cause we know,
3. O! Thou God of all, Hear us when we call, Help us one and all

For the Lord; Gird your ar - mor on, Stand firm, ev - 'ry one; Rest your
Must pre-vail; Shield and banner bright, Gleam-ing in the light; Bat - tling
By Thy grace; When the bat-tle's done, And the vic-t'ry's won, May we

Chorus. ff

cause up - on His ho - ly word.
for the right We ne'er can fail. Rouse, then, sol - diers, ral - ly round the
wear the crown Be - fore Thy face.

ban - ner, Read - y, stead - y, pass the word a - long; On - ward, for - ward,

shout a - loud Ho - san - na! Christ is Cap - tain of the might-y throng. A - MEN.

Under His Wings

William O. Cushing. COPYRIGHT, 1896, BY THE BIGLOW & MAIN CO. USED BY PERMISSION.   Ira D. Sankey.

Solo or Duet.

1. Un - der His wings I am safe - ly a - bid - ing; Tho' the night
2. Un - der His wings, what a ref - uge in sor - row! How the heart
3. Un - der His wings, O what pre - cious en - joy - ment! There will I

deep - ens and tem - pests are wild, Still I can trust Him; I
yearn - ing - ly turns to His rest! Oft - en when earth has no
hide till life's tri - als are o'er; Shel - tered, pro - tect - ed, no

know He will keep me; He has re - deemed me, and I am His child.
balm for my heal - ing, There I find com - fort, and there I am blest.
e - vil can harm me; Rest - ing in Je - sus I'm safe ev - er - more.

CHORUS.

Un - der His wings, un - der His wings, Who from His love can sev - er?

Under His wings my soul shall abide, Safe - ly a - bide for - ev - er. A - MEN.

Satisfied

A. H. Ackley.
WORDS AND MUSIC COPYRIGHT, 1909, BY B. D. ACKLEY.
E. O. EXCELL, OWNER.
B. D. Ackley.

1. When I have fin-ished my pil-grim-age here, When shall have vanished temp-
2. When I am troub-led by grief and de-spair, Grace nev - er - fail-ing a-
3. When I have trav-eled the way with my Lord, Count-ing the mile-posts by

ta - tion and fear, As in the arms of His love I a - bide,
waits me up there; Will-ing to trust Him what - ev - er be - tide,
faith in His word, Liv-ing and dy-ing with Him at my side,

CHORUS.

I shall be sat - is - fied.... I........ shall be sat - is - fied,
I shall be sat is - fied, I shall be sat-is-fied,

I............ shall be sat - is - fied; Shel - tered a-
I shall be sat - is - fied, I shall be sat - is - fied;

rit.

bove by His in - fi - nite love, I shall be sat - is - fied. A - MEN.

Praise Him! Praise Him!

Fanny J. Crosby.   Chester G. Allen.

1. Praise Him! praise Him! Je-sus, our bless-ed Re-deem-er! Sing O Earth, His
2. Praise Him! praise Him! Je-sus, our bless-ed Re-deem-er! For our sins He
3. Praise Him! praise Him! Je-sus, our bless-ed Re-deem-er! Heav'nly por-tals,

won-der-ful love proclaim! Hail Him! hail Him! highest archangels in glo-ry;
suffered, and bled, and died; He our Rock, our hope of e-ter-nal sal-va-tion,
loud with ho-san-nas ring! Je-sus, Sav-ior, reigneth for-ev-er and ev-er;

Strength and hon-or give to His ho-ly name! Like a shep-herd, Je-sus will
Hail Him! hail Him! Je-sus the Cru-ci-fied. Sound His Prais-es! Je-sus who
Crown Him! crown Him! Prophet, and Priest, and King! Christ is coming! over the

REFRAIN.

guard His children, In His arms He carries them all day long: Praise Him! praise Him!
bore our sorrows, Love unbounded, wonderful, deep and strong:
world vic-to-rious, Pow'r and glo-ry un-to the Lord be-long:

tell of His ex-cel-lent greatness; Praise Him! praise Him! ever in joyful song! A-MEN.

Fill My Heart

Dr. M. Victor Staley.

Chas. H. Gabriel.

1. Fill my heart, O bless-ed Sav - ior, With Thy sav-ing grace di - vine;
2. With Thy hand to lead me on-ward, I can nev - er miss the way;
3. When I hear Thy voice so ten - der, In my hours of bit - ter grief,

I would feel Thy lov - ing pres-ence, Sweet as - sur-ance I am Thine.
Tho' at times it may be drear - y I shall nev - er dis-tant stray.
It will cheer me as no oth - er, Bring-ing ev - er sure re - lief.

Wan-d'rer lone-ly, I am call - ing Un - to Thee from out the night;
In the hour when sin-ful pleas-ures Sore - ly tempt me from Thy side,
Sweet-er far than earth-ly mu - sic, Fill - ing all my soul with peace,

FINE.

Lead me by Thy ten-der mer-cy Out of dark - ness in - to light.
Draw me near-er, ev - er near-er, For I would with Thee a - bide.
Are Thy pre-cious words, O Sav-ior, Bid-ding all my sor-rows cease.

D.S.—*Give to me the sweet as - sur-ance That I am a child of Thine.*

CHORUS.

D.S.

Fill my heart, O bless - ed Sav - ior, With Thy saving grace divine; A-MEN.

In His Keeping

C. H. M.

Mrs. C. H. Morris.

1. When the ear-ly morn-ing breaking, Slumber from my eye-lids shaking, Comes the
2. Some-times dark clouds hang o'er me, Not one step I see be - fore me, Still, my
3. Gen - tle e - ven-tide is near-ing, Light from Heaven dis-ap-pear-ing, Still the

bless-ed tho't with wak-ing, I am in His keep-ing. Day ad - van-ces, la - bor
Sav - ior, I a - dore Thee, I am in His keep-ing. I can trust His hand to
bless-ed tho't so cheer-ing, I am in His keep-ing. Now night's curtains gather

bringing, Care, her mantle 'round me flinging, Yet midst all my soul keeps singing,
guide me, 'Neath His wings He'll safely hide me, And no harm can e'er be-tide me,
'round me, Yet its dangers have not found me, For His an-gel guards surround me,

CHORUS.

I am in His care. I am in my Father's keeping, I am in His ten-der

rit.

care; Wheth-er wak-ing, wheth-er sleep-ing, I am in His care. A-MEN.

All the Way My Savior Leads Me

Fanny J. Crosby.   COPYRIGHT, 1917, BY MARY RUNYON LOWRY. RENEWAL.   Robert Lowry.
USED BY PERMISSION.

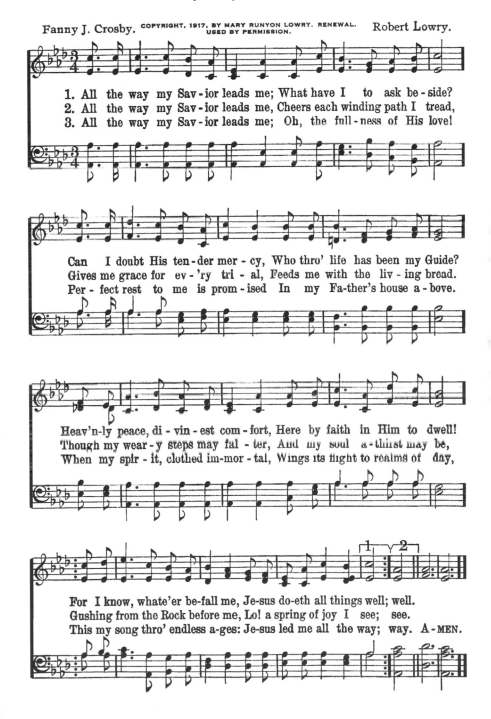

1. All the way my Sav-ior leads me; What have I to ask be-side?
2. All the way my Sav-ior leads me, Cheers each winding path I tread,
3. All the way my Sav-ior leads me; Oh, the full-ness of His love!

Can I doubt His ten-der mer-cy, Who thro' life has been my Guide?
Gives me grace for ev-'ry tri-al, Feeds me with the liv-ing bread.
Per-fect rest to me is prom-ised In my Fa-ther's house a-bove.

Heav'n-ly peace, di-vin-est com-fort, Here by faith in Him to dwell!
Though my wear-y steps may fal-ter, And my soul a-thirst may be,
When my spir-it, clothed im-mor-tal, Wings its flight to realms of day,

For I know, whate'er be-fall me, Je-sus do-eth all things well; well.
Gushing from the Rock before me, Lo! a spring of joy I see; see.
This my song thro' endless a-ges: Je-sus led me all the way; way. A-MEN.

On the Firing Line

On the Firing Line

In un-bro-ken line on to vic-t'ry go, And shoulder to shoulder stand. A-MEN.
In un-bro-ken line on to vic-t'ry go,

O Worship the King

Sir Robert Grant. *Lyons. 10. 11.* Francis Joseph Haydn.

1. O wor-ship the King all-glo-rious a-bove, And grate-ful-ly
2. O tell of His might, and sing of His grace, Whose robe is the
3. Thy boun-ti-ful care what tongue can re-cite? It breathes in the
4. Frail chil-dren of dust, and fee-ble as frail, In Thee do we

sing His won-der-ful love; Our Shield and De-fend-er, the An-cient of
light, whose can o py space; His char-iots of wrath the deep thunder-clouds
air, it shines in the light, It streams from the hills, it de-scends to the
trust, nor find Thee to fail; Thy mer-cies how ten-der! how firm to the

days, Pa-vil-ioned in splen-dor, and gird-ed with praise.
form, And dark is His path on the wings of the storm.
plain, And sweet-ly dis-tills in the dew and the rain.
end! Our Mak-er, De-fend-er, Re-deem-er, and Friend, A-MEN.

The Banner of the Cross

El Nathan.   James McGranahan.

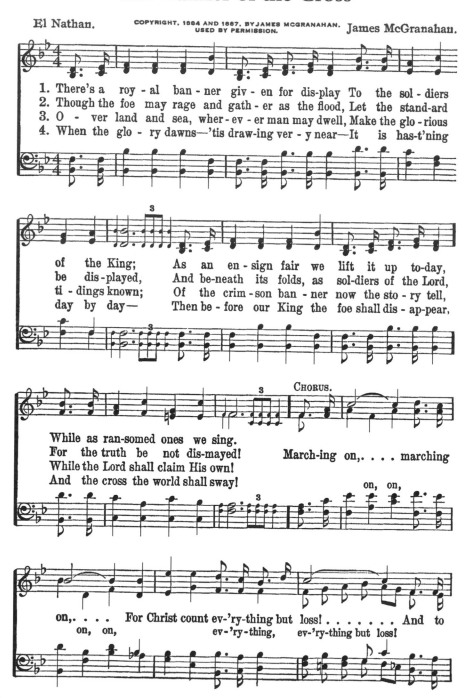

1. There's a roy - al ban - ner giv - en for dis-play To the sol - diers
2. Though the foe may rage and gath - er as the flood, Let the stand-ard
3. O - ver land and sea, wher - ev - er man may dwell, Make the glo - rious
4. When the glo - ry dawns—'tis draw-ing ver - y near—It is has-t'ning

of the King; As an en-sign fair we lift it up to-day,
be dis-played, And be-neath its folds, as sol-diers of the Lord,
ti - dings known; Of the crim-son ban - ner now the sto - ry tell,
day by day— Then be - fore our King the foe shall dis - ap-pear,

CHORUS.

While as ran-somed ones we sing.
For the truth be not dis-mayed!
While the Lord shall claim His own!
And the cross the world shall sway!

March-ing on, ... marching
on, on,

on, ... For Christ count ev-'ry-thing but loss! . . . . And to
on, on,   ev-'ry-thing,   ev-'ry-thing but loss!

The Banner of the Cross

crown Him King, toil and sing 'Neath the ban-ner of the cross! A-MEN.
we'll Be - neath

Lead On, O King Eternal

Ernest W. Shurtleff. *Lancashire.* 7s. 6s. D. Henry Smart.

1. Lead on, O King E - ter - nal, The day of march has come; Henceforth in fields of
2. Lead on, O King E - ter - nal, Till sin's fierce war shall cease, And holiness shall
3. Lead on, O King E - ter - nal, We fol-low, not with fears; For gladness breaks like

con-quest Thy tents shall be our home. Thro' days of prep-a - ra - tion Thy grace has
whis - per The sweet A-men of peace; For not with swords loud clashing, Nor roll of
morn-ing Where'er Thy face appears; Thy cross is lift-ed o'er us; We jour-ney

made us strong, And now, O King E - ter-nal, We lift our bat-tle song.
stir-ring drums; With deeds of love and mercy, The heav'nly kingdom comes.
in its light: The crown awaits the conquest; Lead on, O God of might. A-MEN.

Faith Is the Victory

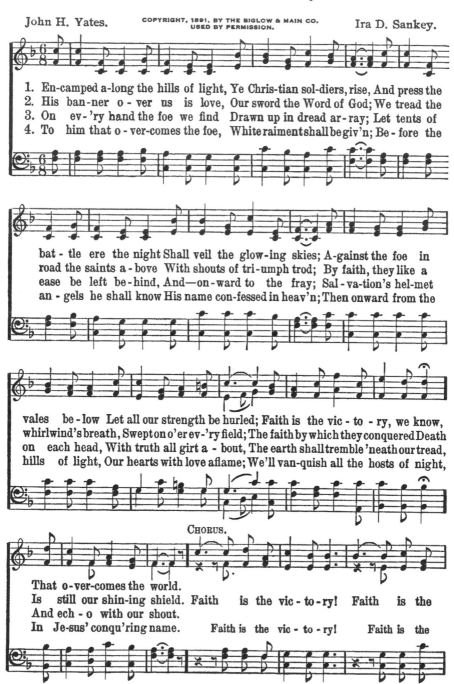

John H. Yates.

Ira D. Sankey.

1. En-camped a-long the hills of light, Ye Chris-tian sol-diers, rise, And press the
2. His ban-ner o-ver us is love, Our sword the Word of God; We tread the
3. On ev-'ry hand the foe we find Drawn up in dread ar-ray; Let tents of
4. To him that o-ver-comes the foe, White raiment shall be giv'n; Be-fore the

bat-tle ere the night Shall veil the glow-ing skies; A-gainst the foe in
road the saints a-bove With shouts of tri-umph trod; By faith, they like a
ease be left be-hind, And—on-ward to the fray; Sal-va-tion's hel-met
an-gels he shall know His name con-fessed in heav'n; Then onward from the

vales be-low Let all our strength be hurled; Faith is the vic-to-ry, we know,
whirlwind's breath, Swept on o'er ev-'ry field; The faith by which they conquered Death
on each head, With truth all girt a-bout, The earth shall tremble 'neath our tread,
hills of light, Our hearts with love aflame; We'll van-quish all the hosts of night,

CHORUS.

That o-ver-comes the world.
Is still our shin-ing shield. Faith is the vic-to-ry! Faith is the
And ech-o with our shout.
In Je-sus' conqu'ring name. Faith is the vic-to-ry! Faith is the

Faith Is the Victory

Hiding in Thee

Rev. Wm. O. Cushing. COPYRIGHT, 1905. BY IRA D. SANKEY. RENEWAL. Ira D. Sankey.

vic-to-ry! Oh, glo-ri-ous vic-to-ry, That o-ver-comes the world. A-MEN.
vic-to-ry!

1. O safe to the Rock that is high-er than I, My soul in its
2. In the calm of the noon-tide, in sor-row's lone hour, In times when temp-
3. How oft in the con-flict, when pressed by the foe, I have fled to my

con-flicts and sor-rows would fly; So sin-ful, so wear-y, Thine, Thine would I
ta-tion casts o'er me its pow'r; In the tempests of life, on its wide, heaving
Ref-uge and breathed out my woe; How oft-en, when tri-als like sea-bil-lows

CHORUS.

be; Thou blest "Rock of A-ges," I'm hid-ing in Thee.
sea, Thou blest "Rock of A-ges," I'm hid-ing in Thee. Hid-ing in Thee,
roll, Have I hid-den in Thee, O Thou Rock of my soul.

Hid-ing in Thee, Thou blest "Rock of A-ges," I'm hid-ing in Thee. A-MEN.

We've a Story to Tell to the Nations

Colin Sterne.   *Sterne. 10. 8. 7. 7. 7.*   H. Ernest Nichol.

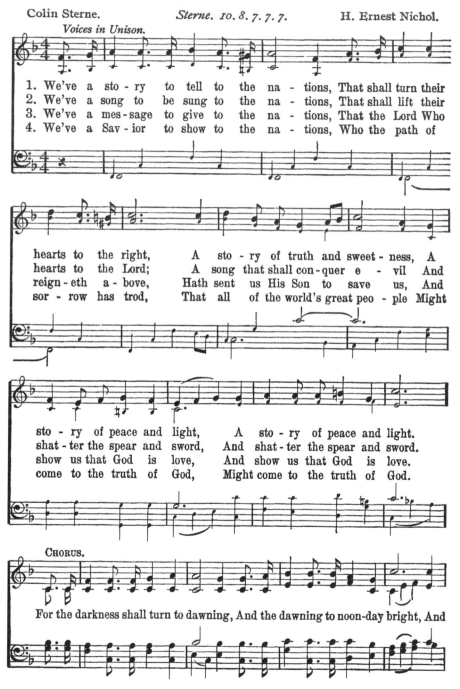

Voices in Unison.

1. We've a sto-ry to tell to the na-tions, That shall turn their
2. We've a song to be sung to the na-tions, That shall lift their
3. We've a mes-sage to give to the na-tions, That the Lord Who
4. We've a Sav-ior to show to the na-tions, Who the path of

hearts to the right,   A sto-ry of truth and sweet-ness, A
hearts to the Lord;   A song that shall con-quer e-vil And
reign-eth a-bove,   Hath sent us His Son to save us, And
sor-row has trod,   That all of the world's great peo-ple Might

sto-ry of peace and light,   A sto-ry of peace and light.
shat-ter the spear and sword,   And shat-ter the spear and sword.
show us that God is love,   And show us that God is love.
come to the truth of God,   Might come to the truth of God.

CHORUS.

For the darkness shall turn to dawning, And the dawning to noon-day bright, And

We've a Story to Tell to the Nations

Christ's great kingdom shall come on earth, The kingdom of love and light. A-MEN.

May Jesus Christ Be Praised

From the German.

Sir Joseph Barnby.

1. When morn-ing gilds the skies, My heart a - wak-ing cries:
2. When sleep her balm de - nies, My si - lent spir - it sighs:
3. Does sad-ness fill my mind, A sol - ace here I find:
4. In Heav'n's e - ter - nal bliss The love-liest strain is this:
5. Be this, while life is mine, My can - ti - cle di - vine,

May Je - sus Christ be praised; A - like at work and prayer
May Je - sus Christ be praised; When e - vil thoughts mo - lest,
May Je - sus Christ be praised; Or fades my earth - ly bliss,
May Je - sus Christ be praised; The pow'rs of dark - ness fear,
May Je - sus Christ be praised; Be this th' e - ter - nal song,

To Je-sus I re - pair: May Je - sus Christ be praised.
With this I shield my breast: May Je - sus Christ be praised.
My com-fort still is this: May Je - sus Christ be praised.
When this sweet chant they hear: May Je - sus Christ be praised.
Thro' all the a - ges on: May Je - sus Christ be praised. A-MEN.

My Savior First of All

Fanny J. Crosby.   COPYRIGHT, 1891, BY JNO. R. SWENEY.   Jno. R. Sweney.

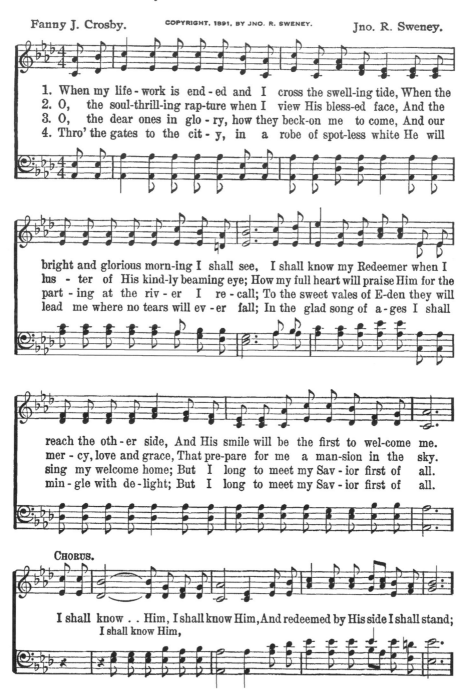

1. When my life-work is end-ed and I cross the swell-ing tide, When the
2. O, the soul-thrill-ing rap-ture when I view His bless-ed face, And the
3. O, the dear ones in glo-ry, how they beck-on me to come, And our
4. Thro' the gates to the cit-y, in a robe of spot-less white He will

bright and glorious morn-ing I shall see, I shall know my Redeemer when I
lus - ter of His kind-ly beaming eye; How my full heart will praise Him for the
part - ing at the riv - er I re - call; To the sweet vales of E-den they will
lead me where no tears will ev - er fall; In the glad song of a-ges I shall

reach the oth - er side, And His smile will be the first to wel-come me.
mer - cy, love and grace, That pre-pare for me a man-sion in the sky.
sing my welcome home; But I long to meet my Sav - ior first of all.
min - gle with de-light; But I long to meet my Sav - ior first of all.

Chorus.

I shall know . . Him, I shall know Him, And redeemed by His side I shall stand;
I shall know Him,

My Savior First of All

I shall know Him, I shall know Him by the print of the nails in His hand. AMEN.
I shall know Him,

Something for Jesus

S. D. Phelps.

Robert Lowry.

1. Sav - ior, Thy dy - ing love Thou gav - est me, Nor should I
2. At the blest mer - cy - seat, Plead-ing for me, My fee - ble
3. Give me a faith-ful heart,—Like-ness to Thee,— That each de-
4. All that I am and have,—Thy gifts so free,— In joy, in

aught with-hold, Dear Lord, from Thee: In love my soul would bow, My heart ful-
faith looks up, Je - sus, to Thee: Help me the cross to bear, Thy wondrous
part - ing day Hence-forth may see Some work of love be - gun, Some deed of
grief, thro' life, Dear Lord, for Thee! And when Thy face I see, My ran-somed

fill its vow, Some of-f'ring bring Thee now, Something for Thee.
love de - clare, Some song to raise, or prayer, Something for Thee
kindness done, Some wand'rer sought and won, Something for Thee.
soul shall be, Thro' all e - ter - ni - ty, Something for Thee. A - MEN.

Linger With Me, Precious Savior

Mrs. E. W. Chapman.

Chas. Edw. Prior.

1. Lin-ger with me, precious Sav-ior, Earthly joys are fad-ing fast;
2. Lin-ger with me, precious Sav-ior, Let the west-ern sun-set's glow,
3. Lin-ger with me, precious Sav-ior, Let Thine arms a-round me fold;

Lending, Lord, Thy grace and fa-vor Till this fleet-ing life has passed.
Rays of bright and shin-ing bril-liance O'er my hap-py spir-it throw.
When the Jor-dan's wave I en-ter Do not then re-lease Thy hold.

Dear-est friends a-round me gath-er, Tho' o'er some the grave has closed;
Light-er, light-er be the eve-ning, When the day of life is done;
When the bright e-ter-nal morning Shall my glad free spir-it wake,

Heed-ing not the i-cy fin-ger, Calm their souls on Thee re-posed.
Dear-er, dear-er be Thy presence With me at the set of sun.
Still be with me, O my Sav-ior, And my soul to glo-ry take.

CHORUS.

Lin-ger with me, precious Sav-ior, Closely hold in Thine my hand;
Linger with me, precious Savior, Closely hold in Thine my hand;

Linger With Me, Precious Savior

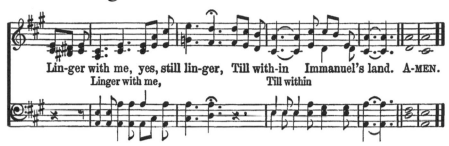

Lin-ger with me, yes, still lin-ger, Till with-in Immanuel's land. A-MEN.
Linger with me,   Till within

It Was His Love

Rev. E. A. Hoffman.   COPYRIGHT, 1915, BY E. O. EXCELL.   Chas. H. Gabriel.
WORDS AND MUSIC.

1. It was His love that reached my soul, It was His grace that made me whole,
2. It was His love, so boundless, free, That moved the Lord to par-don me,
3. It was His love im-pelled my heart To turn from self and sin a-part,
4. It was His great a-maz-ing love So well displayed from Heav'n a-bove,

And now He keeps me day by day, And safe-ly leads me all the way.
And owns me for a ransomed child, Re-deemed, renewed and rec-on-ciled.
And find in Him the wondrous pow'r A Chris-tian life to live each hour.
That bro't to me such peace and rest, And made me so su-preme-ly blest.

D.S.—My heart and life shall sing of Thee In time and in e-ter-ni-ty.

CHORUS.

O wondrous and a-maz-ing love! O grace that saved and ransomed me! AMEN.

Never Give Up

Fanny J. Crosby.

I. Allan Sankey.

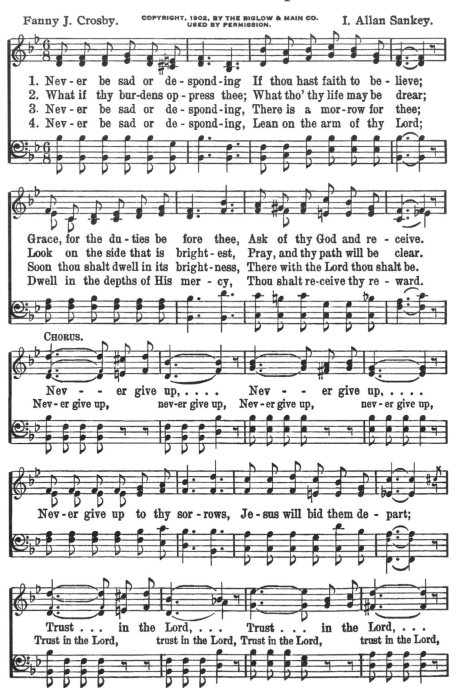

1. Nev-er be sad or de-spond-ing If thou hast faith to be-lieve;
2. What if thy bur-dens op-press thee; What tho' thy life may be drear;
3. Nev-er be sad or de-spond-ing, There is a mor-row for thee;
4. Nev-er be sad or de-spond-ing, Lean on the arm of thy Lord;

Grace, for the du-ties be fore thee, Ask of thy God and re-ceive.
Look on the side that is bright-est, Pray, and thy path will be clear.
Soon thou shalt dwell in its bright-ness, There with the Lord thou shalt be.
Dwell in the depths of His mer-cy, Thou shalt re-ceive thy re-ward.

CHORUS.

Nev - - er give up, ... Nev - - er give up, ...
Nev-er give up, nev-er give up, Nev-er give up, nev-er give up,

Nev-er give up to thy sor-rows, Je-sus will bid them de-part;

Trust ... in the Lord, ... Trust ... in the Lord, ...
Trust in the Lord, trust in the Lord, Trust in the Lord, trust in the Lord,

Never Give Up

Sing when your tri - als are great - est, Trust in the Lord and take heart. A-MEN.

Pass It On

Henry Burton.

Geo. C. Stebbins.

1. Have you had a kind-ness shown? Pass it on; 'Twas not giv'n for
2. Did you hear the lov-ing word—Pass it on; Like the sing-ing
3. 'Twas the sun-shine of a smile—Pass it on; Stay-ing but a
4. Have you found the heav'nly light? Pass it on; Souls are grop-ing
5. Be not self-ish in thy greed, Pass it on; Look up-on thy

thee a - lone, Pass it on; Let it trav - el down the years, Let it
of a bird? Pass it on; Let its mu - sic live and grow, Let it
lit - tle while! Pass it on; A - pril beam, the lit - tle thing, Still it
in the night, Daylight gone; Hold thy lighted lamp on high, Be a
brother's need, Pass it on; Live for self, you live in vain; Live for

wipe an-oth-er's tears, Till in heav'n the deed appears—Pass it on.
cheer an-oth-er's woe, You have reaped what others sow, Pass it on.
wakes the flow'rs of spring, Makes the silent birds to sing—Pass it on.
star in some one's sky, He may live who else would die, Pass it on.
Christ, you live a - gain; Live for Him, with Him you reign—Pass it on. A - MEN.

The Whole Wide World for Jesus

Will. L. Thompson.

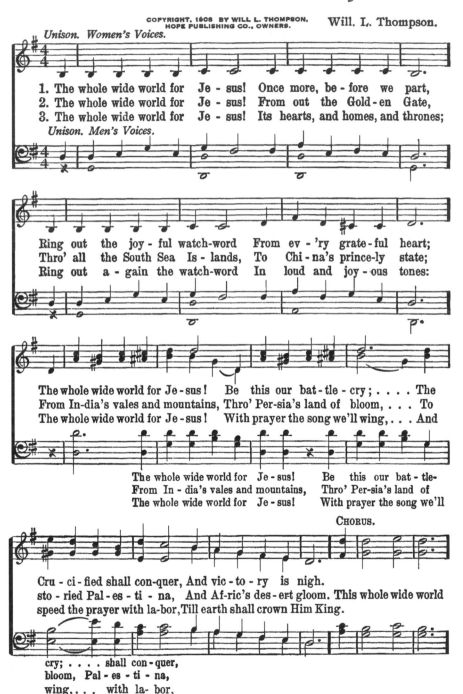

Unison. Women's Voices.

1. The whole wide world for Je - sus! Once more, be - fore we part,
2. The whole wide world for Je - sus! From out the Gold - en Gate,
3. The whole wide world for Je - sus! Its hearts, and homes, and thrones;

Unison. Men's Voices.

Ring out the joy - ful watch-word From ev - 'ry grate - ful heart;
Thro' all the South Sea Is - lands, To Chi - na's prince - ly state;
Ring out a - gain the watch-word In loud and joy - ous tones:

The whole wide world for Je - sus! Be this our bat - tle - cry; .... The
From In-dia's vales and mountains, Thro' Per-sia's land of bloom, ... To
The whole wide world for Je - sus! With prayer the song we'll wing, ... And

The whole wide world for Je - sus! Be this our bat - tle-
From In - dia's vales and mountains, Thro' Per-sia's land of
The whole wide world for Je - sus! With prayer the song we'll

CHORUS.

Cru - ci - fied shall con - quer, And vic - to - ry is nigh.
sto - ried Pal - es - ti - na, And Af-ric's des - ert gloom. This whole wide world
speed the prayer with la - bor, Till earth shall crown Him King.

cry; .... shall con - quer,
bloom, Pal - es - ti - na,
wing, ... with la - bor,

The Whole Wide World for Jesus

For Je-sus! for Je-sus! This whole wide world For Je-sus Christ, our Lord. A-MEN.

I Want to Live Closer to Jesus

Jessie Brown Pounds. COPYRIGHT, 1906, BY CHAS. H. GABRIEL. Chas. H. Gabriel.
E. O. EXCELL, OWNER.

1. I want to live clos - er to Je - sus,— My vis - ion so
2. I want to live clos - er to Je - sus, For of - ten I
3. I want to live clos - er to Je - sus, Still clos - er and

oft - en is dim; To look on His face and be filled with His grace,
fol - low a - far; His voice I would hear sound-ing close to my ear
clos - er each day; Till clasp-ing His hand I shall en - ter the land

D. S.—*To look on His face and be filled with His grace,*
FINE. CHORUS.

I want to live clos - er to Him.
To tell what His prom - is - es are. Clos - er to Je - sus,
Where I shall be near Him for aye.

I want to live clos - er to Him. D. S.

clos - er to Je - sus, Clos - er to Him I would be: A - MEN.

Wonderful Savior

COPYRIGHT, 1909, BY E. O. EXCELL.

J. W. MacGill.   Arr. by E. O. Excell.

1. Je - sus has loved me—won - der - ful Sav - ior! Je - sus has
2. Je - sus has saved me—won - der - ful Sav - ior! Je - sus has
3. Je - sus will lead me—won - der - ful Sav - ior! Je - sus will
4. Je - sus will crown me—won - der - ful Sav - ior! Je - sus will

loved me, I can - not tell why; He came to res - cue sin - ners un-
saved me, I can - not tell how; But this I do know, He came, my
lead me, I can - not tell where; So I will fol - low thro' joy or
crown me, I can - not tell when; White throne of splen - dor hail I with

wor - thy, My heart He con - quered, for Him I would die.
ran - som, Dy - ing on Cal - v'ry, with thorns on His brow.
sor - row, Sun - shine or tem - pest, since He leads me there.
glad - ness, Crowned in the pres - ence of an - gels and men. A - MEN.

Of Christ the Savior

The Lord Jesus Christ, by His perfect obedience, and sacrifice of Himself, which He, through the eternal Spirit, once offered up unto God, hath fully satisfied the justice of His Father; and purchased, not only reconciliation, but an everlasting inheritance in the kingdom of heaven, for all those who the Father hath given unto Him.   *The Westminster Confession of Faith* (WCF) 8.5

Where Hast Thou Gleaned Today?

P. P. Bliss.

P. P. Bliss.

Question.

1. Wear- y glean-er, whence comest thou, With emp-ty hands and cloud-ed brow?
2. Care-less glean-er, what hast thou here, These fad-ed flow'rs and leaf-lets sere?
3. Bur-dened gleaner, thy sheaves I see; In-deed thou must a-wear-y be!

Plod-ding a-long thy lone-ly way, Tell me, where hast thou gleaned to-day?
Hun-gry and thirst-y, tell me, pray, Where, oh, where hast thou gleaned to-day?
Sing-ing a-long the homeward way, Glad one, where hast thou gleaned to-day?

Answer.

Late I found a bar-ren field, The har-vest past, my search re-vealed
All day long in sha-dy bow'rs, I've gai-ly sought earth's fairest flow'rs;
Stay me not, till day is done I've gath-ered hand fuls one by one;

Oth-ers gold-en sheaves had gained, On-ly stub-ble for me re-mained.
Now, a-las! too late I see All I've gath-ered is van-i-ty.
Here and there for me they fall, Close by the reap-ers I've found them all.

CHORUS.

Forth to the har-vest-field a-way! Gath-er your hand-fuls while you may;

Count Your Blessings

Rev. Johnson Oatman, Jr.   COPYRIGHT, 1897, BY E. O. EXCELL.   E. O. Excell.
WORDS AND MUSIC.

1. When up-on life's bil-lows you are tem - pest-tossed, When you are dis-
2. Are you ev - er bur-dened with a load   of   care? Does the cross seem
3. When you look at oth-ers with their lands and   gold, Think that Christ has
4. So,   a - mid the con-flict, whether great   or   small, Do not be dis-

cour-aged, think-ing all   is   lost, Count your man-y bless-ings,name them
heav - y you are called to   bear? Count your man-y bless-ings, ev - 'ry
prom-ised you His wealth un - told; Count your man-y bless-ings, mon-ey
cour-aged, God is   o - ver   all; Count your man-y bless-ings, an-gels

one   by   one, And it will sur-prise you what the Lord hath   done.
doubt will   fly, And you will be sing-ing as the days go   by.
can - not   buy Your re-ward in Heav-en, nor your home on   high.
will   at - tend, Help and com-fort give you to your jour-ney's   end.

CHORUS.

Count   your bless-ings, Name them one by   one; Count   your
Count your man-y   bless-ings,   Name them one by one;   Count your man-y

bless-ings, See what God   hath   done; Count   your bless-ings,
bless-ings,   See what God hath done; Count your man-y   bless-ings,

Count Your Blessings

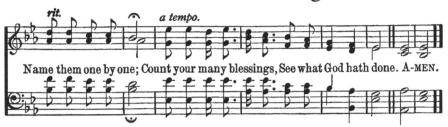

Name them one by one; Count your many blessings, See what God hath done. A-MEN.

'Tis So Sweet to Trust in Jesus

Louisa M. R. Stead.   COPYRIGHT, 1882 AND 1910, BY WM. J. KIRKPATRICK. USED BY PER.   Wm. J. Kirkpatrick.

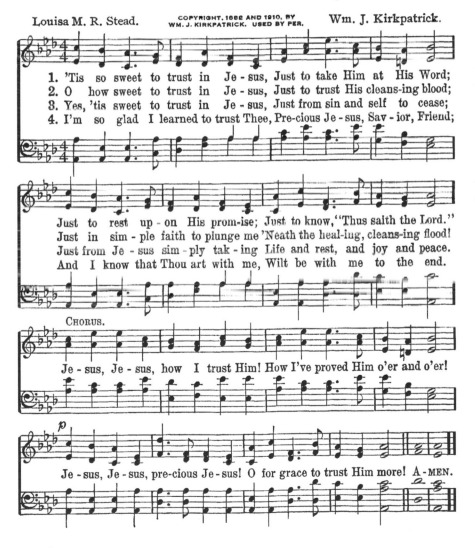

1. 'Tis so sweet to trust in Je-sus, Just to take Him at His Word;
2. O how sweet to trust in Je-sus, Just to trust His cleans-ing blood;
3. Yes, 'tis sweet to trust in Je-sus, Just from sin and self to cease;
4. I'm so glad I learned to trust Thee, Pre-cious Je-sus, Sav-ior, Friend;

Just to rest up-on His prom-ise; Just to know, "Thus saith the Lord."
Just in sim-ple faith to plunge me 'Neath the heal-ing, cleans-ing flood!
Just from Je-sus sim-ply tak-ing Life and rest, and joy and peace.
And I know that Thou art with me, Wilt be with me to the end.

CHORUS.

Je-sus, Je-sus, how I trust Him! How I've proved Him o'er and o'er!

Je-sus, Je-sus, precious Je-sus! O for grace to trust Him more! A-MEN.

More Like the Master

C. H. G.

Chas. H. Gabriel.

1. More like the Mas-ter I would ev-er be, More of His meek-ness, more hu-mil-i-ty; More zeal to la-bor, more cour-age to be true, More con-se-cra-tion for work He bids me do. . . . . . Take Thou my heart, . . I would be Thine a-lone; . . Take Thou my heart . . and make it all Thine own; . . Purge me from sin, . . . O Lord, I now im-

2. More like the Mas-ter is my dai-ly prayer; More strength to car-ry cross-es I must bear; More ear-nest ef-fort to bring His kingdom in; More of His Spir-it, the wan-der-er to win. . . . . Take my heart, O take my heart, I would be Thine a-lone; Take my heart, O take my heart and make it all Thine own; Purge Thou me from ev'ry sin, O Lord,

3. More like the Mas-ter I would live and grow; More of His love to oth-ers I would show; More self-de-ni-al, like His in Gal-i-lee, More like the Mas-ter I long to ev-er be. . . . .

rit.   CHORUS.

More Like the Master

plore, .. Wash me and keep .. me Thine for-ev-er-more. A - MEN.
now im-plore, Wash and keep, O wash and keep me Thine for-ev-er-more.

O Love That Wilt Not Let Me Go

George Matheson.   *Margaret. 8. 8. 8. 8. 6.*   A. L. Peace.

1. O Love that wilt not let me go,   I   rest my wear-y soul in
2. O Light that fol-l'west all my way,   I   yield my flick'ring torch to
3. O Joy that seek-est me thro' pain,   I   can-not close my heart to
4. O Cross that lift-est up my head,   I   dare not ask to hide from

Thee;   I   give Thee back the life I   owe,   That in Thine
Thee;   My heart re-stores its bor-rowed ray,   That in Thy
Thee;   I   trace the rain-bow thro' the rain,   And feel the
Thee;   I   lay in dust life's glo-ry dead,   And from the

o - cean depths its flow   May rich - er,   full - er   be.
sun-shine's glow its day   May bright-er,   fair - er   be.
prom - ise is not vain   That morn shall tear - less   be.
ground there blossoms red   Life that shall end - less   be.   A - MEN.

The Joyful Song

Fanny J. Crosby.

Adam Geibel.

1. Be - hold! a roy - al ar - my, With ban - ner, sword and shield, Is
2. And now the foe, ad - vanc - ing, That val - iant host as - sails, And
3. Oh, when the war is end - ed, When strife and con - flict cease, When

marching forth to con - quer, On life's great bat - tle-field; Its ranks are
yet they nev - er fal - ter, Their cour-age nev - er fails; Their Lead-er
all are safe - ly gath - ered With - in the vale of peace, Be - fore the

filled with sol - diers, U - ni - ted, bold and strong, Who fol - low their Com-
calls, "Be faith-ful!" They pass the word a - long, They see His sig - nal
King e - ter - nal, That vast and might-y throng Shall praise His name for-

CHORUS. *In unison.*

mand - er, And sing their joy - ful song.
flash - ing, And shout the joy - ful song. Vic - to - ry, vic - to - ry, Thro'
ev - er, And this shall be their song:

Him that re-deemed us! Vic - to - ry, vic-to-ry, Thro' Je-sus Christ our Lord!

The Joyful Song

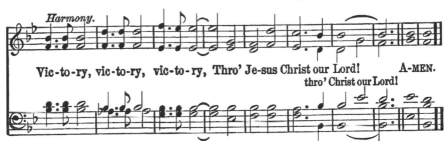

Vic-to-ry, vic-to-ry, vic-to-ry, Thro' Je-sus Christ our Lord!   A-MEN.
thro' Christ our Lord!

Lord, I Hear of Showers of Blessings

Elizabeth Codner.   *Even Me. 8.7.8.7.3.*   William B. Bradbury.

1. Lord, I hear of show'rs of bless-ing Thou art scat-t'ring full and free;
2. Pass me not, O gra-cious Fa-ther, Sin-ful though my heart may be;
3. Pass me not, O ten-der Sav-ior, Let me love and cling to Thee;
4. Love of God, so pure and changeless, Blood of Christ, so rich, so free,

Show'rs, the thirst-y land re-fresh-ing; Let some drops now fall on me,
Thou mightst leave me, but the rather Let Thy mer-cy light on me,
I am long-ing for Thy fa-vor; Whilst Thou'rt calling, O call me,
Grace of God, so strong and boundless, Mag-ni-fy them all in me,

E-ven me, E-ven me, Let some drops now fall on me.
E-ven me, E-ven me, Let Thy mer-cy light on me.
E-ven me, E-ven me, Whilst Thou'rt calling, O call me.
E-ven me, E-ven me, Mag-ni-fy them all in me. A-MEN.

Lead Me Gently Home, Father

W. L. T.   COPYRIGHT PROPERTY OF HOPE PUBLISHING CO.   W. L. Thompson.

1. Lead me gen-tly home, Fa-ther, Lead me gen-tly home,   When life's toils are
2. Lead me gen-tly home, Fa-ther, Lead me gen-tly home,   In life's dark-est

end - ed, And part-ing days have come; Sin no more shall tempt me, Ne'er from
hours, Father, When life's troubles come; Keep my feet from wand'ring, Lest from

Thee I'll roam,   If Thou'lt on - ly lead me, Fa-ther, Lead me gen-tly home.
Thee I'll roam,   Lest I   fall up - on the way-side, Lead me gen-tly home.

CHORUS.

Lead me gen - tly home,   Fa-ther, lead me gen - tly
Lead me gen - tly   home,   Fa - ther, Lead me   gen - tly   home,   Fa - ther.

Lead Me Gently Home, Father

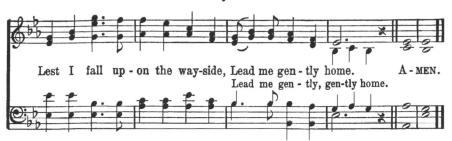

Lest I fall up-on the way-side, Lead me gen-tly home. A-MEN.
Lead me gen - tly, gen-tly home.

Have Thine Own Way, Lord

A. A. P.

Geo. C. Stebbins.

Slowly.

1. Have Thine own way, Lord! Have Thine own way! Thou art the
2. Have Thine own way, Lord! Have Thine own way! Search me and
3. Have Thine own way, Lord! Have Thine own way! Wound-ed and
4. Have Thine own way, Lord! Have Thine own way! Hold o'er my

Pot - ter; I am the clay. Mould me and make me Aft - er Thy
try me, Mas - ter, to - day! Whit - er than snow, Lord, Wash me just
wear - y, Help me, I pray! Pow - er—all pow - er—Sure - ly is
be - ing Ab - so - lute sway! Fill with Thy Spir - it Till all shall

will, While I am wait - ing, Yield-ed and still.
now, As in Thy pres - ence Hum - bly I bow.
Thine! Touch me and heal me, Sav - ior di - vine!
see Christ on - ly, al - ways, Liv - ing in me! A - MEN.

O Where Are the Reapers?

Eben E. Rexford.

George F. Root.

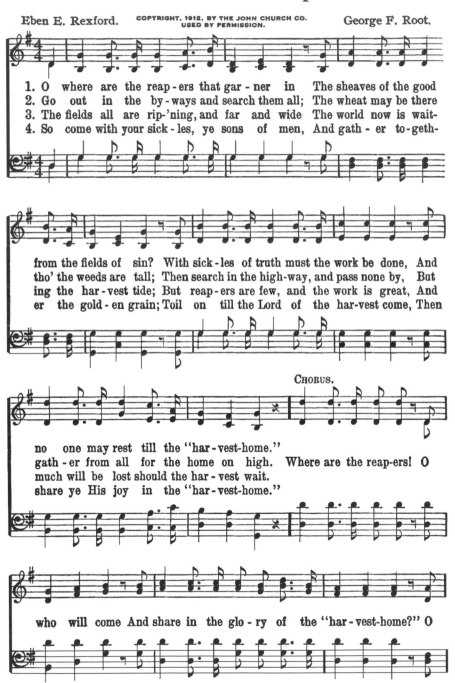

1. O where are the reap-ers that gar-ner in The sheaves of the good from the fields of sin? With sick-les of truth must the work be done, And no one may rest till the "har-vest-home."

2. Go out in the by-ways and search them all; The wheat may be there tho' the weeds are tall; Then search in the high-way, and pass none by, But gath-er from all for the home on high.

3. The fields all are rip-'ning, and far and wide The world now is wait-ing the har-vest tide; But reap-ers are few, and the work is great, And much will be lost should the har-vest wait.

4. So come with your sick-les, ye sons of men, And gath-er to-geth-er the gold-en grain; Toil on till the Lord of the har-vest come, Then share ye His joy in the "har-vest-home."

Chorus.

Where are the reap-ers! O who will come And share in the glo-ry of the "har-vest-home?" O

O Where Are the Reapers?

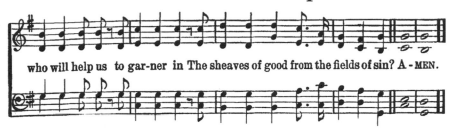

who will help us to gar-ner in The sheaves of good from the fields of sin? A - MEN.

I Gave My Life for Thee

Frances R. Havergal. COPYRIGHT, 1916, BY THE JOHN CHURCH CO.   P. P. Bliss.

1. I gave My life for thee, My pre-cious blood I shed,
2. My Fa-ther's house of light, My glo-ry - cir - cled throne
3. I suf-fered much for thee, More than thy tongue can tell,
4. And I have brought to thee, Down from My home a - bove,

That thou might'st ransomed be, And quick-ened from the dead;
I left, for earth - ly night, For wand'rings sad and lone;
Of bit-t'rest ag - o - ny, To res - cue thee from hell;
Sal - va - tion full and free, My par - don and My love;

I gave, I gave My life for thee, What hast thou given for Me?
I left, I left it all for thee, Hast thou left aught for Me?
I've borne, I've borne it all for thee, What hast thou borne for Me?
I bring, I bring rich gifts to thee, What hast thou brought to Me?   A - MEN.

Oh, What a Change!

Ada R. Habershon. COPYRIGHT. 1905, BY CHARLES M. ALEXANDER. INTERNATIONAL COPYRIGHT SECURED. Robert Harkness.

1. Soon will our Sav - ior from Heav-en ap - pear; Sweet is the hope and its pow-er to cheer; All will be changed by a glimpse of His face— This is the goal at the end of our race!

2. Lone - li - ness changed to re - un - ion com - plete, Ab - sence ex - changed for a place at His feet, Sleeping ones raised in a mo-ment of time, Liv - ing ones changed to His im - age sub - lime!

3. Sun - rise will chase all the dark-ness a - way, Night will be changed to the brightness of day, Tempest will change to in - ef - fa - ble calm, Weep-ing will change to a ju - bi - lant psalm!

4. Weakness will change to mag - nif - i - cent strength, Fail - ure will change to per - fec-tion at length, Sor-row will change to un - end -ing de - light, Walk-ing by faith change to walk-ing by sight!

CHORUS.

Oh, what a change, ... Oh, what a change, ... When I shall
Oh, what a change, Oh, what a change,

see His won-der-ful face! Oh, what a change, ... Oh, what a
Oh, what a change,

Oh, What a Change!

change, ... When I shall see His face! A-MEN.
Oh, what a change,

Nearer, Still Nearer

C. H. M. COPYRIGHT, 1898, BY H. L. GILMOUR. WENONAH, N. J. USED BY PERMISSION. Mrs. C. H. Morris.

1. Near-er, still near-er, close to Thy heart, Draw me, my Savior, so precious Thou
2. Near-er, still near-er, noth-ing I bring, Naught as an off'ring to Je-sus my
3. Near-er, still near-er, Lord, to be Thine, Sin, with its fol-lies, I glad-ly re-
4. Near-er, still near-er, while life shall last, Till safe in glo-ry my an-chor is

art; Fold me, O fold me close to Thy breast, Shel-ter me safe in that
King; On-ly my sin-ful, now con-trite heart, Grant me the cleansing Thy
sign; All of its pleasures, pomp and its pride, Give me but Je-sus, my
cast; Thro' end-less a-ges, ev-er to be, Near-er, my Sav-ior, still

"Ha-ven of Rest," Shel-ter me safe in that "Ha-ven of Rest."
blood doth im-part, Grant me the cleansing Thy blood doth impart.
Lord cru-ci-fied, Give me but Je-sus, my Lord cru-ci-fied.
near-er to Thee, Near-er, my Sav-ior, still near-er to Thee. A-MEN.

Do You Wonder Why?

Mrs. C. D. Martin.　　COPYRIGHT, 1906, BY CHAS. H. GABRIEL.　　Chas. H. Gabriel.
　　　　　　　　　　　　E. O. EXCELL, OWNER.

1. Do you won-der why I love Him And would make His glo-ries known?
2. Do you won-der why I serve Him, Why the cross I glad-ly bear,
3. Do you won-der why I praise Him, When you view His wound-ed side,

If you saw His deep com-pas-sion As to me it has been shown,
Why the work of His great king-dom I so love with Him to share?
And the cross on which He suf-fered And for me was cru-ci-fied?

You would won-der why a mo-ment I could cease to sing His praise,
If you felt the yoke up-on you That He gives me now to wear,
When you read re-demp-tion's sto-ry, As re-cord-ed in His word,

You would love Him and a-dore Him For the won-ders of His grace!
You would won-der that I ev-er Bore a-lone my load of care!
You will then no lon-ger won-der Why I praise my bless-ed Lord.

CHORUS.

Oh, that I . . . . could on-ly tell you, Tell you
Oh, that I could on-ly tell you, Oh, that I could on-ly tell you, Tell you

Do You Wonder Why?

why . . . . . He loves me so, ... Why He par - - doned my trans-
why He loves me so, tell you why He loves me so, Why He pardoned my transgressions, why He

gres - sions, Why He washed . . . me white as snow. A - MEN.
pardoned my transgressions, Why He washed me white as snow, why He washed me white as snow.

I Love Him

English Hymn Book.   USED BY PERMISSION.   S. C. Foster.

1. Gone from my heart the world and all its charm; Gone are my sins and
2. Once I was lost up - on the plains of sin; Once was a slave to
3. Once I was bound, but now I am set free; Once I was blind, but

all that would a - larm; Gone ev - er-more, and by His grace I know The
doubts and fears with-in; Once was a-fraid to trust a lov-ing God, But
now the light I see; Once I was dead, but now in Christ I live, To

D. S.—*Be-cause He first loved me, And*
FINE.   D. S.

pre-cious blood of Je - sus cleanses white as snow.
now my guilt is washed a-way in Je - sus' blood. I love Him, I love Him,
tell the world the peace that He a - lone can give.   A - MEN.

purchased my sal-va - tion on Cal-v'ry's tree.

Reapers Are Needed

Lizzie DeArmond.   COPYRIGHT, 1910, BY E. O. EXCELL WORDS AND MUSIC.   Samuel W. Beazley.

1. Hark to the mu-sic re-sound-ing, Reap-ers are need-ed to-day;
2. For-ward with hearts full of glad-ness, Reap-ers, I pray you, make haste;
3. Hark to the song they are sing-ing! See, they have treasures so rare;

Fields are all white, to the har-vest Let us be up and a-way!
Grain there is read-y and wait-ing, If not soon gath-ered, will waste;
Soon will the har-vest be end-ed, Haste, then, their tro-phies to share.

Ev-er the Mas-ter is call-ing, Has-ten! the shad-ows are fall-ing;
Then let us hear you re-ply-ing, La-bor with cour-age un-dy-ing,
Let no one be i-dly dream-ing, Look! look! the har-vest is gleam-ing,

On to the har-vest-field, Gath-er the gold-en yield, Pre-cious sheaves.
Send up a word of cheer, Tell of the rest so near, Rest at home.
Join ye the reap-ing band, Lend them a help-ing hand, Ere the night.

Chorus or Quartet.

Hark! hark! comes the song, On! on! join the throng; Forth with joyful, lov-ing heart,

Reapers Are Needed

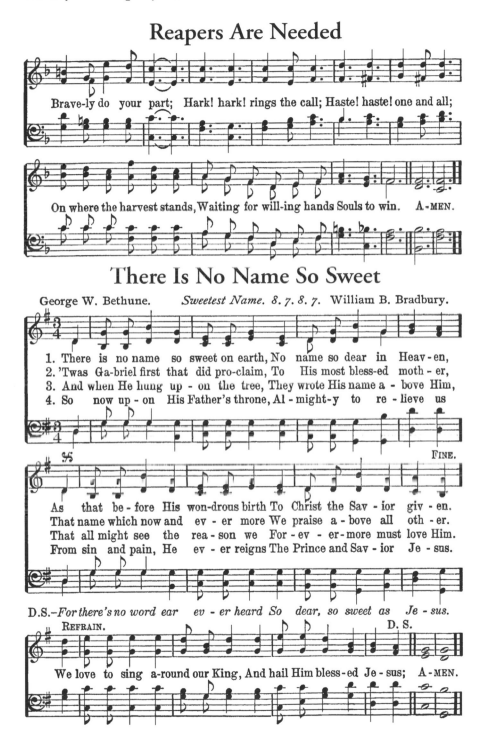

Brave-ly do your part; Hark! hark! rings the call; Haste! haste! one and all;

On where the harvest stands, Waiting for will-ing hands Souls to win.   A-MEN.

There Is No Name So Sweet

George W. Bethune.   *Sweetest Name. 8. 7. 8. 7.*   William B. Bradbury.

1. There is no name   so sweet on earth, No   name so dear   in Heav-en,
2. 'Twas Ga-briel first that did pro-claim, To   His most bless-ed moth-er,
3. And when He hung up - on the tree, They wrote His name a - bove Him,
4. So   now up - on His Father's throne, Al - might-y to re - lieve us

FINE.

As   that be - fore His won-drous birth To Christ the Sav - ior giv - en.
That name which now and ev - er more We praise a - bove all   oth - er.
That all might see   the rea - son we For - ev - er-more must love Him.
From sin and pain, He ev - er reigns The Prince and Sav - ior Je - sus.

D.S.–*For there's no word ear   ev - er heard So   dear, so sweet as   Je - sus.*

REFRAIN.   D. S.

We love to sing a-round our King, And hail Him bless-ed Je - sus;   A-MEN.

His Eye Is on the Sparrow

Mrs. C. D. Martin.

Chas. H. Gabriel.

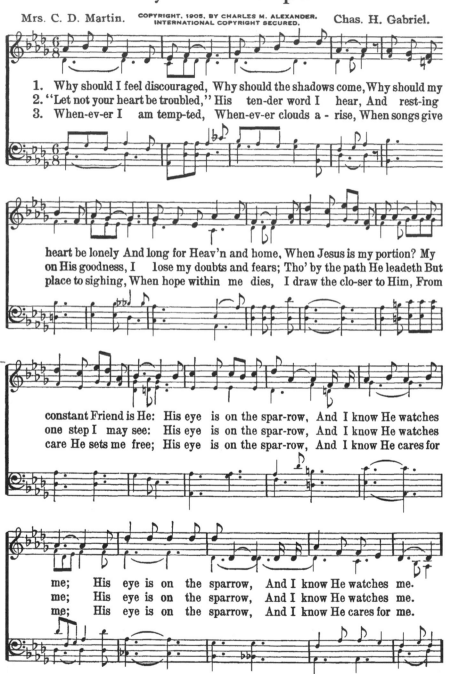

1. Why should I feel discouraged, Why should the shadows come, Why should my
2. "Let not your heart be troubled," His ten-der word I hear, And rest-ing
3. When-ev-er I am temp-ted, When-ev-er clouds a-rise, When songs give

heart be lonely And long for Heav'n and home, When Jesus is my portion? My
on His goodness, I lose my doubts and fears; Tho' by the path He leadeth But
place to sighing, When hope within me dies, I draw the clo-ser to Him, From

constant Friend is He: His eye is on the spar-row, And I know He watches
one step I may see: His eye is on the spar-row, And I know He watches
care He sets me free; His eye is on the spar-row, And I know He cares for

me; His eye is on the sparrow, And I know He watches me.
me; His eye is on the sparrow, And I know He watches me.
me; His eye is on the sparrow, And I know He cares for me.

His Eye Is on the Sparrow

CHORUS.

I sing be-cause I'm hap-py,(I'm happy,) I sing be-cause I'm free,(I'm free,)

rall.

For His eye is on the spar-row, And I know He watches me.   A - MEN.

The Call for Reapers

J. O. Thompson.

J. B. O. Clemm.

1. Far and near the fields are teem-ing With the waves of ri-pened grain;
2. Send them forth with morn's first beaming; Send them in the noontide's glare;
3. O thou, whom thy Lord is send-ing, Gath-er now the sheaves of gold;

FINE.

Far and near their gold is gleam-ing O'er the sun-ny slope and plain.
When the sun's last rays are gleam-ing, Bid them gath-er ev-'ry-where.
Heav'nward then at eve-ning wend-ing, Thou shalt come with joy un-told.

D. S.—*Send them now the sheaves to gath-er, Ere the har-vest-time pass by.*

CHORUS.   D. S.

Lord of har-vest, send forth reapers! Hear us, Lord, to Thee we cry; A-MEN.

Soldiers of Jesus

William M. Runyan.
Harry Dixon Loes.

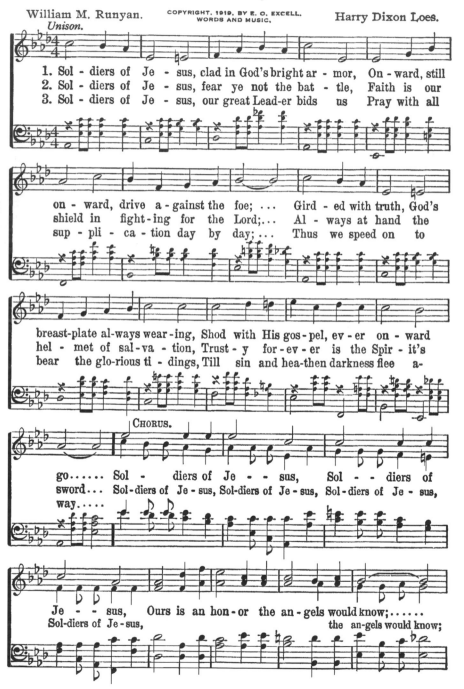

1. Sol - diers of Je - sus, clad in God's bright ar - mor, On - ward, still
2. Sol - diers of Je - sus, fear ye not the bat - tle, Faith is our
3. Sol - diers of Je - sus, our great Lead-er bids us Pray with all

on - ward, drive a - gainst the foe; ... Gird - ed with truth, God's
shield in fight-ing for the Lord; ... Al - ways at hand the
sup - pli - ca - tion day by day; ... Thus we speed on to

breast-plate al-ways wear-ing, Shod with His gos-pel, ev - er on - ward
hel - met of sal - va - tion, Trust - y for - ev - er is the Spir - it's
bear the glo-rious ti - dings, Till sin and hea-then darkness flee a-

CHORUS.

go...... Sol - diers of Je - - sus, Sol - - diers of
sword... Sol-diers of Je - sus, Sol-diers of Je - sus, Sol-diers of Je - sus,
way.....

Je - - sus, Ours is an hon - or the an-gels would know; ......
Sol-diers of Je - sus,   the an-gels would know;

Soldiers of Jesus

Herald of glory, Herald of glory, Herald of glory, Guardians of freedom,
Herald of glory, Guard-ians of free-dom,

free-dom, Sol-diers of Je-sus, ev-er on-ward go. A-MEN.
guard-ians of free-dom,

Everything for Jesus

Flora E. Breck.

Chas. H. Gabriel.

1. Ev-'ry-thing for Je-sus! Un-to Him I give All I have and hope for;
2. Ev-'ry-thing for Je-sus! I will con-se-crate Life and love and ser-vice,
3. Ev-'ry-thing for Je-sus! Ev-'ry-thing I know, On my lov-ing Sav-ior

CHORUS.

'Tis for Him I live.
Ere it be too late. Ev-'ry-thing for Je-sus, All to Christ my King!
Glad-ly I be-stow.

To Him who gave so much for me, I will give Him ev-'ry-thing. A-MEN.

The Fight Is On

C. H. M.   COPYRIGHT, 1905, BY WM. J. KIRKPATRICK.   Mrs. C. H. Morris.

1. The fight is on, the trump-et sound is ring-ing out, The cry "To
2. The fight is on, a-rouse, ye sol-diers brave and true! Je-ho-vah
3. The Lord is lead-ing on to cer-tain vic-to-ry; The bow of

arms!" is heard a-far and near; The Lord of hosts is march-ing
leads, and vic-t'ry will as-sure; Go, buck-le on the ar-mor
prom-ise spans the east-ern sky; His glo-rious name in ev-'ry

on to vic-to-ry, The tri-umph of the Christ will soon ap-pear.
God has giv-en you, And in His strength un-to the end en-dure.
land shall hon-ored be; The morn will break, the dawn of peace is nigh.

CHORUS. *Unison.*

The fight is on, O Chris-tian sol-dier, And face to face in stern ar-ray,

With

ar-mor gleaming, and colors streaming, The right and wrong engage to-day!

The Fight Is On

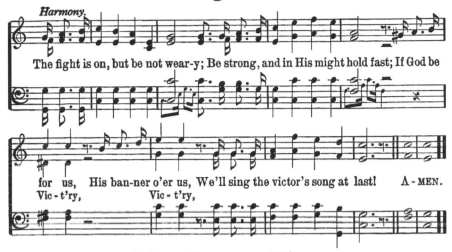

The fight is on, but be not wear-y; Be strong, and in His might hold fast; If God be
for us, His ban-ner o'er us, We'll sing the victor's song at last! A-MEN.
Vic-t'ry, Vic-t'ry,

More Love to Thee

Elizabeth Prentiss.   USED BY PERMISSION.   W. H. Doane.

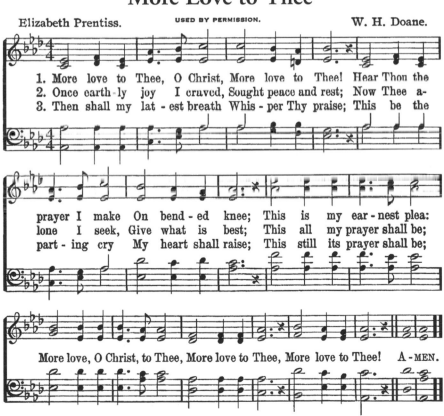

1. More love to Thee, O Christ, More love to Thee! Hear Thou the
2. Once earth-ly joy I craved, Sought peace and rest; Now Thee a-
3. Then shall my lat-est breath Whis-per Thy praise; This be the

prayer I make On bend-ed knee; This is my ear-nest plea:
lone I seek, Give what is best; This all my prayer shall be;
part-ing cry My heart shall raise; This still its prayer shall be;

More love, O Christ, to Thee, More love to Thee, More love to Thee! A-MEN.

I Love to Tell the Story

Katherine Hankey.   *Hankey. 7s. D.*   William G. Fischer.

1. I love to tell the sto - ry, Of un - seen things a - bove,
2. I love to tell the sto - ry; More won - der - ful it seems
3. I love to tell the sto - ry; 'Tis pleas - ant to re - peat
4. I love to tell the sto - ry; For those who know it best

Of Je - sus and His glo - ry, Of Je - sus and His love.
Than all the gold - en fan - cies Of all our gold - en dreams.
What seems, each time I tell it, More won - der - ful - ly sweet.
Seem hun - ger - ing and thirst - ing To hear it, like the rest.

I love to tell the sto - ry Be - cause I know 'tis true;
I love to tell the sto - ry, It did so much for me;
I love to tell the sto - ry, For some have nev - er heard
And when in scenes of glo - ry I sing the new, new song,

It sat - is - fies my long - ings As noth - ing else can do.
And that is just the rea - son I tell it now to thee.
The mes - sage of sal - va - tion From God's own Ho - ly Word.
'Twill be the old, old sto - ry That I have loved so long.

I Love to Tell the Story

REFRAIN.

I love to tell the sto - ry, 'Twill be my theme in glo - ry To tell the old, old sto - ry, Of Je - sus and His love. A-MEN.

My Prayer

P. P. Bliss.

COPYRIGHT, 1915. USED BY PER. THE JOHN CHURCH CO., OWNERS OF THE COPYRIGHT.

P. P. Bliss.

1. More ho - li - ness give me, More striv-ing with-in; More pa-tience in
2. More grat-i-tude give me, More trust in the Lord; More pride in His
3. More pu - ri - ty give me, More strength to o'er-come; More free-dom from

suf - f'ring, More sor - row for sin; More faith in my Sav - ior,
glo - ry, More hope in His word; More tears for His sor - rows,
earth-stains, More long-ings for home; More fit for the king-dom,

rit.

More sense of His care; More joy in His ser-vice, More purpose in prayer.
More pain at His grief; More meekness in tri - al, More praise for relief.
More used would I be; More bless-ed and ho - ly, More, Savior, like Thee. A-MEN.

To the Work

Fanny J. Crosby.

W. H. Doane.

1. To the work! to the work! we are serv-ants of God, Let us
2. To the work! to the work! let the hun-gry be fed; To the
3. To the work! to the work! there is la-bor for all; For the
4. To the work! to the work! in the strength of the Lord, And a

fol-low the path that our Mas-ter has trod; With the balm of His
foun-tain of life let the wear-y be led; In the cross and its
king-dom of dark-ness and er-ror shall fall; And the name of Je-
robe and a crown shall our la-bor re-ward; When the home of the

coun-sel our strength to re-new, Let us do with our might what our
ban-ner our glo-ry shall be, While we her-ald the ti-dings, "Sal-
ho-vah ex-alt-ed shall be, In the loud-swell-ing cho-rus, "Sal-
faith-ful our dwell-ing shall be, And we shout with the ran-somed, "Sal-

CHORUS.

hands find to do.
va - tion is free!" Toil-ing on, toil-ing on,
va - tion is free!"
va - tion is free!" Toil-ing on, toil-ing on,

To the Work

Toil-ing on,   toil-ing on;   Let us hope,
Toil-ing on,   toil - ing on;   and trust,

let us watch,   And la - bor till the Mas-ter comes. A-MEN.
   and pray,

Pass Me Not

Fanny J. Crosby.   COPYRIGHT PROPERTY OF FANNIE T. DOANE.   W. H. Doane.

1. Pass me not, O gen-tle Sav-ior, Hear my hum-ble cry; While on oth-ers
2. Let me at a throne of mer-cy Find a sweet re-lief; Kneel-ing there in
3. Trust-ing on-ly in Thy mer-it, Would I seek Thy face; Heal my wounded,
4. Thou the Spring of all my com-fort, More than life to me, Whom have I on

CHORUS.

Thou art call-ing, Do not pass me by.
deep con-tri-tion, Help my un-be-lief. Sav-ior, Sav-ior, Hear my hum-ble
bro-ken spir-it, Save me by Thy grace.
earth beside Thee? Whom in Heav'n but Thee?

cry; While on oth-ers Thou art call-ing, Do not pass me by.   A-MEN.

Where Cross the Crowded Ways of Life

F. Mason North.   *Germany. L. M.*   Beethoven.

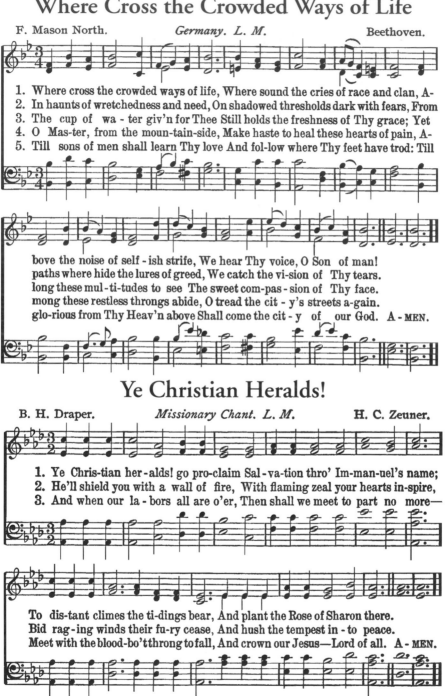

1. Where cross the crowded ways of life, Where sound the cries of race and clan, A-
2. In haunts of wretchedness and need, On shadowed thresholds dark with fears, From
3. The cup of wa-ter giv'n for Thee Still holds the freshness of Thy grace; Yet
4. O Mas-ter, from the moun-tain-side, Make haste to heal these hearts of pain, A-
5. Till sons of men shall learn Thy love And fol-low where Thy feet have trod: Till

bove the noise of self - ish strife, We hear Thy voice, O Son of man!
paths where hide the lures of greed, We catch the vi-sion of Thy tears.
long these mul-ti-tudes to see The sweet com-pas-sion of Thy face.
mong these restless throngs abide, O tread the cit - y's streets a-gain.
glo-rious from Thy Heav'n above Shall come the cit - y of our God. A - MEN.

Ye Christian Heralds!

B. H. Draper.   *Missionary Chant. L. M.*   H. C. Zeuner.

1. Ye Chris-tian her-alds! go pro-claim Sal-va-tion thro' Im-man-uel's name;
2. He'll shield you with a wall of fire, With flaming zeal your hearts in-spire,
3. And when our la - bors all are o'er, Then shall we meet to part no more—

To dis-tant climes the ti-dings bear, And plant the Rose of Sharon there.
Bid rag-ing winds their fu-ry cease, And hush the tempest in - to peace.
Meet with the blood-bo't throng to fall, And crown our Jesus—Lord of all. A - MEN.

Give Me Jesus

Fanny J. Crosby.

COPYRIGHT, 1879, BY JNO. R. SWENEY.
USED BY PERMISSION OF L. E. SWENEY, EXECUTRIX.

Jno. R. Sweney.

1. Take the world, but give me Je - sus,—All its joys are but a name;
2. Take the world, but give me Je - sus, Sweet-est com - fort of my soul;
3. Take the world, but give me Je - sus, Let me view His con-stant smile;
4. Take the world, but give me Je - sus; In His cross my trust shall be,

But His love a - bid - eth ev - er, Thro' e - ter - nal years the same.
With my Sav - ior watch-ing o'er me, I can sing tho' bil - lows roll.
Then thro'-out my pil - grim jour - ney Light will cheer me all the while.
Till, with clear - er, bright - er vi - sion, Face to face my Lord I see.

D.S.—*Oh, the full - ness of re - demp - tion, Pledge of end - less life a - bove!*

CHORUS.

D. S.

Oh, the height and depth of mer-cy! Oh, the length and breadth of love! A - MEN.

The Love of God our Savior

… The kindness and love of God our Savior toward man appeared, not by works of righteousness which we have done, but according to His mercy He saved us, by the washing of regeneration, and renewing of the Holy Ghost; which He shed on us abundantly through Jesus Christ our Savior; that being justified by His grace, we should be made heirs according to the hope of eternal life.

Titus 3: 4–6

Faith of Our Fathers

Frederick W. Faber.   *St. Catherine. L. M. 6l.*   H. F. Hemy.

1. Faith of our fa - thers! liv - ing still In spite of dun-geon, fire, and sword:
2. Our fa-thers, chained in pris-ons dark, Were still in heart and conscience free:
3. Faith of our fa - thers! we will love Both friend and foe in all our strife:

O how our hearts beat high with joy When-e'er we hear that glo-rious word!
How sweet would be their children's fate, If they, like them, could die for thee!
And preach thee, too, as love knows how, By kind-ly words and vir-tuous life:

Faith of our fa-thers! ho-ly faith! We will be true to thee till death!
Faith of our fa-thers! ho-ly faith! We will be true to thee till death!
Faith of our fa-thers! ho-ly faith! We will be true to thee till death! A - MEN.

How Firm a Foundation

George Keith.   *Foundation. 11s.*   Anne Steele.

1. How firm a foun - da - tion, ye saints of the Lord, Is laid for your
2. "Fear not, I am with thee, O be not dis-mayed, For I am thy
3. "When thro' the deep wa-ters I call thee to go, The riv - ers of
4. "When thro' fier-y tri - als thy path-way shall lie, My grace, all-suf-

How Firm a Foundation

faith in His ex - cel - lent Word! What more can He say than to
God, I will still give thee aid; I'll strength-en thee, help thee, and
sor - row shall not o - ver - flow; For I will be with thee thy
fi - cient, shall be thy sup - ply; The flames shall not hurt thee, I

you He hath said, To you, who for ref - uge to Je-sus have fled?
cause thee to stand, Up - held by My gra-cious, om-nip - o-tent hand.
tri - als to bless, And sanc - ti - fy to thee thy deep-est dis-tress.
on - ly de - sign Thy dross to con-sume, and thy gold to re - fine." A-MEN.

[Second Tune.]   *Portuguese Hymn. 11s.*   Unknown.

1. How firm a foun - da-tion, ye saints of the Lord, Is laid for your faith in His

ex - cel - lent Word! What more can He say than to you He hath said, To you, who for

ref - uge to Je - sus have fled? To you, who for ref-uge to Je-sus have fled? A-MEN.

All Hail the Power of Jesus' Name

E. Perronet.   *Diadem. C. M.*   James Ellor.

1. All hail the pow'r of Je - sus' name! Let an-gels pros-trate fall,
2. Ye cho - en seed of Is - rael's race, Ye ransomed from the fall,
3. Let ev - 'ry kin - dred, ev - 'ry tribe, On this ter - res - trial ball,
4. O that with yon - der sa - cred throng We at His feet may fall,

Let an - gels pros-trate fall; Bring forth the roy - al di - a - dem,
Ye ran-somed from the fall, Hail Him who saves you by His grace,
On this ter - res - trial ball, To Him all maj - es - ty as - cribe,
We at His feet may fall! We'll join the ev - er - last - ing song,

And crown . . . . Him, Crown Him,

And crown Him, crown Him, crown Him, crown Him, And crown Him Lord of
And crown . . . . Him, Crown Him,

And crown Him, crown Him, crown Him, Crown . . . .

crown Him, crown Him;

all, crown Him; And crown Him Lord of all! A - MEN.
crown . . . . . Him;

. . . . Him; And crown Him Lord of all!

All Hail the Power

[Second Tune.]   *Coronation. C. M.*   Oliver Holden.

1. All hail the pow'r of Je - sus' name! Let an - gels pros-trate fall;
2. Ye cho - sen seed of Is - rael's race, Ye ran-somed from the fall,
3. Let ev - 'ry kin-dred, ev - 'ry tribe On this ter - res - trial ball,

Bring forth the roy - al di - a - dem, And crown Him Lord of all,
Hail Him who saves you by His grace, And crown Him Lord of all,
To Him all maj - es - ty as - cribe, And crown Him Lord of all,

Bring forth the roy - al di - a - dem, And crown Him Lord of all!
Hail Him who saves you by His grace, And crown Him Lord of all!
To Him all maj - es - ty as - cribe, And crown Him Lord of all! A-MEN.

[Third Tune.]   *Miles' Lane. C. M.*   William Shrubsole.

1. All hail the pow'r of Je-sus' name! Let an-gels pros-trate fall; Bring forth the roy-al

di - a-dem, And crown Him, crown Him, crown Him, Crown Him Lord of all! A-MEN.

Savior, More Than Life

Fanny J. Crosby.

W. H. Doane.

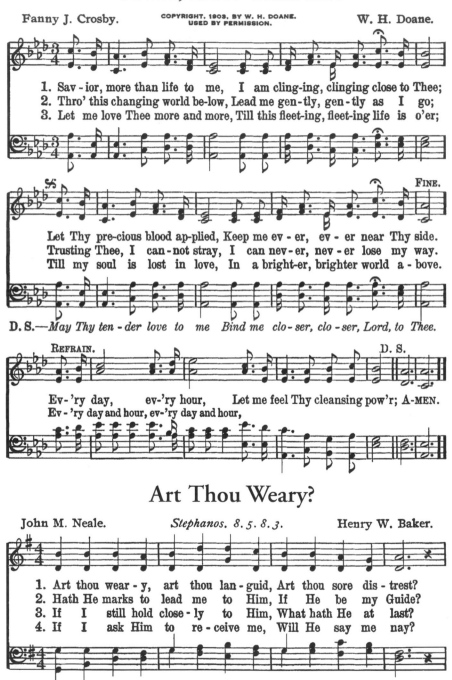

1. Sav-ior, more than life to me, I am cling-ing, clinging close to Thee;
2. Thro' this changing world be-low, Lead me gen-tly, gen-tly as I go;
3. Let me love Thee more and more, Till this fleet-ing, fleet-ing life is o'er;

Let Thy pre-cious blood ap-plied, Keep me ev-er, ev-er near Thy side.
Trusting Thee, I can-not stray, I can nev-er, nev-er lose my way.
Till my soul is lost in love, In a bright-er, brighter world a-bove.

D. S.—May Thy ten-der love to me Bind me clo-ser, clo-ser, Lord, to Thee.

REFRAIN.

Ev-'ry day, ev-'ry hour, Let me feel Thy cleansing pow'r; A-MEN.
Ev-'ry day and hour, ev-'ry day and hour,

Art Thou Weary?

John M. Neale.

Stephanos. 8.5.8.3.

Henry W. Baker.

1. Art thou wear-y, art thou lan-guid, Art thou sore dis-trest?
2. Hath He marks to lead me to Him, If He be my Guide?
3. If I still hold close-ly to Him, What hath He at last?
4. If I ask Him to re-ceive me, Will He say me nay?

Art Thou Weary?

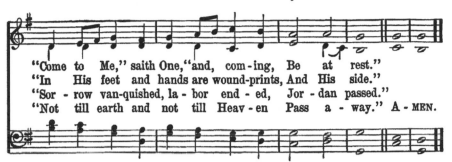

"Come to Me," saith One, "and, com-ing, Be at rest."
"In His feet and hands are wound-prints, And His side."
"Sor-row van-quished, la-bor end-ed, Jor-dan passed."
"Not till earth and not till Heav-en Pass a-way." A-MEN.

Let the Lower Lights Be Burning

P. P. B. USED BY PERMISSION. P. P. Bliss.

1. Bright-ly beams our Fa-ther's mer-cy From His light-house ev-er-more,
2. Dark the night of sin has set-tled, Loud the an-gry bil-lows roar;
3. Trim your fee-ble lamp, my broth-er: Some poor sail-or tem-pest tossed,

But to us He gives the keep-ing Of the lights a-long the shore.
Ea-ger eyes are watch-ing, long-ing, For the lights a-long the shore.
Try-ing now to make the har-bor, In the dark-ness may be lost.

D. S.—*Some poor fainting, strug-gling sea-man You may res-cue, you may save.*

CHORUS. D.S.

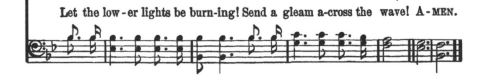

Let the low-er lights be burn-ing! Send a gleam a-cross the wave! A-MEN.

More About Jesus

E. E. Hewitt.   COPYRIGHT, 1915, BY MRS. L. E. SWENEY IN RENEWAL.   Jno. R. Sweney.

1. More a - bout Je - sus would I know, More of His grace to oth - ers show;
2. More a - bout Je - sus let me learn, More of His ho - ly will dis - cern;
3. More a - bout Je - sus; in His word, Hold-ing com-mun-ion with my Lord;
4. More a - bout Je - sus on His throne, Rich-es in glo - ry all His own;

More of His sav - ing full - ness see, More of His love who died for me.
Spir - it of God, my teach-er be, Show-ing the things of Christ to me.
Hear-ing His voice in ev - 'ry line, Mak-ing each faith-ful say - ing mine.
More of His kingdom's sure in-crease; More of His com-ing, Prince of Peace

FINE.

D. S.—*More of His sav - ing full - ness see, More of His love who died for me.*

REFRAIN.   D. S.

More, more a - bout Je - sus, More, more a - bout Je - sus;   A - MEN.

Of Christ the Mediator

It pleased God, in His eternal purpose, to choose and ordain the Lord Jesus, His only begotten Son, to be the Mediator between God and man, the Prophet, Priest, and King, the Head and Savior of His Church, the Heir of all things, and Judge of the world: unto whom He did from all eternity give a people, to be His seed, and to be by Him in time redeemed, called, justified, sanctified, and glorified.   WCF 8.1

My Faith Looks Up to Thee

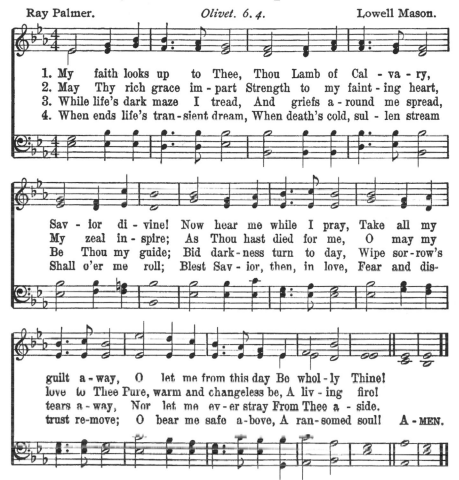

Ray Palmer.   *Olivet. 6. 4.*   Lowell Mason.

1. My faith looks up to Thee, Thou Lamb of Cal-va-ry,
2. May Thy rich grace im-part Strength to my faint-ing heart,
3. While life's dark maze I tread, And griefs a-round me spread,
4. When ends life's tran-sient dream, When death's cold, sul-len stream

Sav-ior di-vine! Now hear me while I pray, Take all my
My zeal in-spire; As Thou hast died for me, O may my
Be Thou my guide; Bid dark-ness turn to day, Wipe sor-row's
Shall o'er me roll; Blest Sav-ior, then, in love, Fear and dis-

guilt a-way, O let me from this day Be whol-ly Thine!
love to Thee Pure, warm and changeless be, A liv-ing fire!
tears a-way, Nor let me ev-er stray From Thee a-side.
trust re-move; O bear me safe a-bove, A ran-somed soul! A-MEN.

The Just Shall Live by Faith

For I am not ashamed of the gospel of Christ: for it is the power of God unto salvation to everyone that believeth; to the Jews first, and also to the Greek.

For therein is the righteousness of God revealed from faith to faith: as it is written, The just shall live by faith.

Romans 1:16–17

Walk in the Light

Bernard Barton.   *Manoah. C. M.*   From Francis J. Haydn.

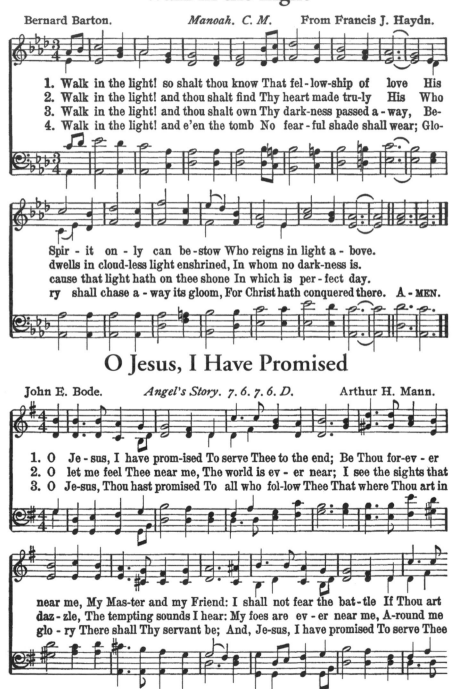

1. Walk in the light! so shalt thou know That fel-low-ship of love His
2. Walk in the light! and thou shalt find Thy heart made tru-ly His Who
3. Walk in the light! and thou shalt own Thy dark-ness passed a-way, Be-
4. Walk in the light! and e'en the tomb No fear-ful shade shall wear; Glo-

Spir-it on-ly can be-stow Who reigns in light a-bove.
dwells in cloud-less light enshrined, In whom no dark-ness is.
cause that light hath on thee shone In which is per-fect day.
ry shall chase a-way its gloom, For Christ hath conquered there. A-MEN.

O Jesus, I Have Promised

John E. Bode.   *Angel's Story. 7. 6. 7. 6. D.*   Arthur H. Mann.

1. O Je-sus, I have prom-ised To serve Thee to the end; Be Thou for-ev-er
2. O let me feel Thee near me, The world is ev-er near; I see the sights that
3. O Je-sus, Thou hast promised To all who fol-low Thee That where Thou art in

near me, My Mas-ter and my Friend: I shall not fear the bat-tle If Thou art
daz-zle, The tempting sounds I hear: My foes are ev-er near me, A-round me
glo-ry There shall Thy servant be; And, Je-sus, I have promised To serve Thee

O Jesus, I Have Promised

by my side, Nor wan-der from the pathway If Thou wilt be my Guide.
and with-in; But, Je-sus, draw Thou near-er, And shield my soul from sin.
to the end; O give me grace to fol - low My Mas-ter and my Friend. A-MEN.

Majestic Sweetness Sits Enthroned

Samuel Stennett.   Ortonville. C. M.   Thomas Hastings.

1. Ma - jes - tic sweet-ness sits en-throned Up - on the Sav - ior's
2. No mor - tal can with Him com - pare, A - mong the sons of
3. He saw me plunged in deep dis - tress, And flew to my re -
4. To Him I owe my life and breath, And all the joys I

brow; His head with ra - diant glo - ries crowned, His lips with
men; Fair - er is He than all the fair Who fill the
lief; For me He bore the shame - ful cross, And car - ried
have; He makes me tri - umph o - ver death, And saves me

grace o'er - flow, His lips with grace o'er - flow.
heav'n-ly train, Who fill the heav'n-ly train.
all my grief, And car - ried all my grief.
from the grave, And saves me from the grave. A - MEN.

Blest Be the Ties

John Fawcett.   *Dennis. S. M.*   Hans G. Naegeli.

1. Blest be the tie that binds Our hearts in Chris-tian love; The fel - low-
2. Be - fore our Fa-ther's throne, We pour our ar-dent prayers; Our fears, our
3. We share our mu - tual woes, Our mu - tual bur-dens bear; And oft - en
4. When we a - sun - der part, It gives us in - ward pain; But we shall

ship of kin - dred minds Is like to that a - bove.
hopes, our aims are one, Our com - forts and our cares.
for each oth - er flows The sym - pa - thiz - ing tear.
still be joined in heart, And hope to meet a - gain. A - MEN.

Jesus, Savior, Pilot Me

Edward Hopper.   *Pilot. 6. 7.*   J. E. Gould.

1. Je - sus, Sav - ior, pi - lot me O - ver life's tem-pes-tuous sea:
2. As a moth - er stills her child, Thou canst hush the o - cean wild;
3. When at last I near the shore, And the fear - ful break-ers roar

Un-known waves be-fore me roll, Hid - ing rocks and treach'rous shoal;
Boist'rous waves o - bey Thy will When Thou say'st to them "Be still!"
'Twixt me and the peace-ful rest, Then, while lean-ing on Thy breast,

Jesus, Savior, Pilot Me

Chart and compass come from Thee, Je - sus, Sav - ior, pi - lot me.
Wondrous Sovereign of the sea, Je - sus, Sav - ior, pi - lot me.
May I hear Thee say to me, "Fear not, I will pi - lot thee." A-MEN.

Revive Us Again

Wm. P. Mackay. John J. Husband.

1. We praise Thee, O God! for the Son of Thy love, For Je-sus who
2. We praise Thee, O God! for Thy Spir-it of light, Who has shown us our
3. All glo-ry and praise to the Lamb that was slain, Who has borne all our
4. Re-vive us a-gain; fill each heart with Thy love; May each soul be re-

CHORUS.

died, and is now gone a - bove.
Sav - ior, and scat-tered our night. Hal-le - lu-jah! Thine the glo-ry, Hal-le-
sins, and hath cleansed ev-'ry stain.
kin-dled with fire from a - bove.

lu-jah! a-men; Hal-le-lu-jah! Thine the glo-ry, re-vive us a-gain. A-MEN.

Thou Art Worthy, O Lord

And the four beasts had each of them six wings about him; and they were full of eyes within: and they rest not day and night, saying, Holy, holy, holy, Lord God Almighty, which was, and is, and is to come.

And when those beasts give glory and honour and thanks to him that sat on the throne' who liveth for ever and ever,

The four and twenty elders fall down before him that sat on the throne, and worship him that liveth for ever and ever, and cast their crowns before the throne, saying,

Thou art worthy, O Lord, to receive glory and honour and power: for thou hast created all things, and for thy pleasure they are and were created.

Revelation 4:8–11

Holy, Holy, Holy

Reginald Heber.   *Nicæa. 11. 12. 12. 10.*   Rev. John B. Dykes.

1. Ho-ly, Ho-ly, Ho-ly,   Lord   God Al-might-y!   Ear-ly in the
2. Ho-ly, Ho-ly, Ho-ly!   All the saints a-dore Thee, Cast-ing down their
3. Ho-ly, Ho-ly, Ho-ly!   Tho' the darkness hide Thee, Tho' the eye of
4. Ho-ly, Ho-ly, Ho-ly,   Lord   God Al-might-y!   All Thy works shall

morn - ing our song shall rise to Thee;   Ho-ly, Ho-ly, Ho-ly!
gold-en crowns a-round the glass-y   sea;   Cher-u-bim and ser-a-phim
sin - ful man Thy glo-ry may not see,   On-ly Thou art ho-ly;
praise Thy name, in earth, and sky, and sea;   Ho-ly, Ho-ly, Ho-ly!

Holy, Holy, Holy

Mer - ci - ful and Might - y! God in Three Per - sons, blessed Trin - i - ty!
fall-ing down be-fore Thee, Who wert, and art, and ev-er-more shalt be.
there is none be-side Thee Per - fect in pow'r, in love, and pu - ri - ty.
Mer - ci - ful and Might - y! God in Three Per - sons, blessed Trin-i - ty! A-MEN.

Come, Thou Almighty King

Anonymous.   *Italian Hymn. 6s. 4s.*   Felice de Giardini.

1. Come, Thou Al - might - y King, Help us Thy name to sing,
2. Come, Thou In - car - nate Word, Gird on Thy might - y sword,
3. Come, Ho - ly Com - fort - er, Thy sa - cred wit - ness bear
4. To the great One in Three E - ter - nal prais - es be

Help us to praise: Fa - ther, all - glo - ri - ous, O'er all vic-
Our prayer at - tend: Come, and Thy peo - ple bless, And give Thy
In this glad hour: Thou who al - might-y art, Now rule in
Hence ev - er - more. His sov-'reign maj - es - ty May we in

to - ri - ous, Come, and reign o - ver us, An-cient of Days.
word suc-cess: Spir - it of ho - li - ness, On us de - scend.
ev - 'ry heart, And ne'er from us de-part, Spir - it of pow'r.
glo - ry see, And to e - ter - ni - ty Love and a - dore. A - MEN.

Where He Leads Me

E. W. Blandly.

COPYRIGHT, 1890, BY J. S. NORRIS.
USED BY PERMISSION.

J. S. Norris.

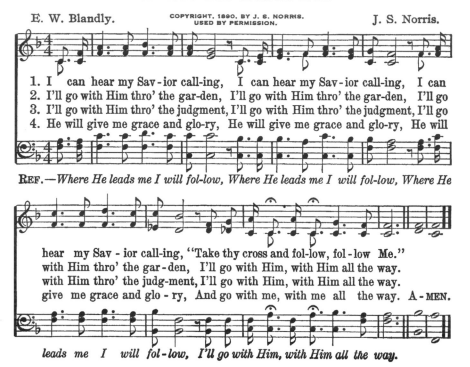

1. I can hear my Sav-ior call-ing, I can hear my Sav-ior call-ing, I can
2. I'll go with Him thro' the gar-den, I'll go with Him thro' the gar-den, I'll go
3. I'll go with Him thro' the judgment, I'll go with Him thro' the judgment, I'll go
4. He will give me grace and glo-ry, He will give me grace and glo-ry, He will

REF.—*Where He leads me I will fol-low, Where He leads me I will fol-low, Where He*

hear my Sav - ior call-ing, "Take thy cross and fol-low, fol-low Me."
with Him thro' the gar-den, I'll go with Him, with Him all the way.
with Him thro' the judg-ment, I'll go with Him, with Him all the way.
give me grace and glo - ry, And go with me, with me all the way. A - MEN.

leads me I will fol-low, I'll go with Him, with Him all the way.

Take Up Your Cross

Then said Jesus unto his disciples, If any man will come after me, let him deny himself, and take up his cross, and follow me.

For whosoever will save his life shall lose it: and whosoever will lose his life for my sake shall find it.

For what is a man profited, if he shall gain the whole world, and lose his own soul? or what shall a man give in exchange for his soul?

For the Son of man shall come in the glory of his Father with his angels; and then he shall reward every man according to his works.

Matthew 16:24–27

Just for Today

E. R. Wilberforce.   H. R. Palmer.

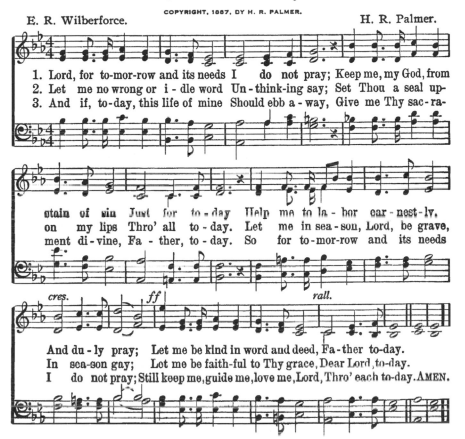

1. Lord, for to-mor-row and its needs I do not pray; Keep me, my God, from
2. Let me no wrong or i - dle word Un - think-ing say; Set Thou a seal up-
3. And if, to-day, this life of mine Should ebb a - way, Give me Thy sac-ra-

otain of sin Just for to - day Help me to la - bor ear - nest-ly.
on my lips Thro' all to - day. Let me in sea - son, Lord, be grave,
ment di - vine, Fa - ther, to - day. So for to-mor-row and its needs

cres.   *ff*   *rall.*

And du - ly pray; Let me be kind in word and deed, Fa - ther to-day.
In sea-son gay; Let me be faith-ful to Thy grace, Dear Lord, to-day.
I do not pray; Still keep me, guide me, love me, Lord, Thro' each to-day. AMEN.

Thou Art My Rock

In thee, O Lord, do I put my trust; let me never be ashamed:
deliver me in thy righteousness.

Bow down thine ear to me; deliver me speedily; be thou my
strong rock, for an house of defence to save me.

For thou art my rock and my fortress; therefore for thy name's
sake lead me, and guide me.

Psalm 31:1–3

In the Cross of Christ

Sir John Bowring.   *Rathbun. 8s. 7s.*   Ithamar Conkey.

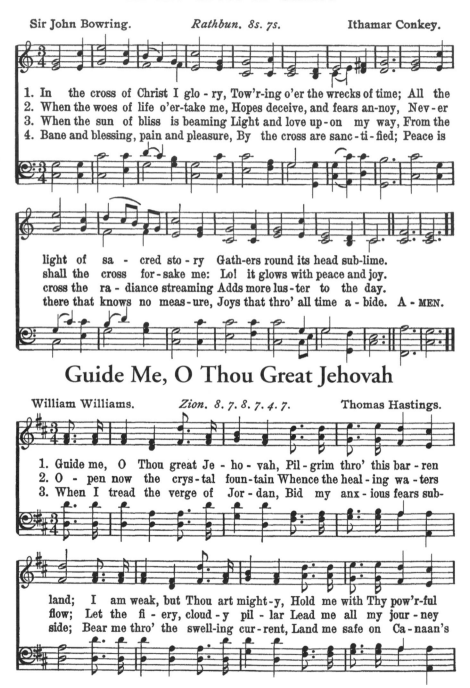

1. In the cross of Christ I glo-ry, Tow'r-ing o'er the wrecks of time; All the
2. When the woes of life o'er-take me, Hopes deceive, and fears an-noy, Nev-er
3. When the sun of bliss is beaming Light and love up-on my way, From the
4. Bane and blessing, pain and pleasure, By the cross are sanc-ti-fied; Peace is

light of sa-cred sto-ry Gath-ers round its head sub-lime.
shall the cross for-sake me: Lo! it glows with peace and joy.
cross the ra-diance streaming Adds more lus-ter to the day.
there that knows no meas-ure, Joys that thro' all time a-bide. A-MEN.

Guide Me, O Thou Great Jehovah

William Williams.   *Zion. 8. 7. 8. 7. 4. 7.*   Thomas Hastings.

1. Guide me, O Thou great Je-ho-vah, Pil-grim thro' this bar-ren
2. O-pen now the crys-tal foun-tain Whence the heal-ing wa-ters
3. When I tread the verge of Jor-dan, Bid my anx-ious fears sub-

land; I am weak, but Thou art might-y, Hold me with Thy pow'r-ful
flow; Let the fi-ery, cloud-y pil-lar Lead me all my jour-ney
side; Bear me thro' the swell-ing cur-rent, Land me safe on Ca-naan's

Guide Me, O Thou Great Jehovah

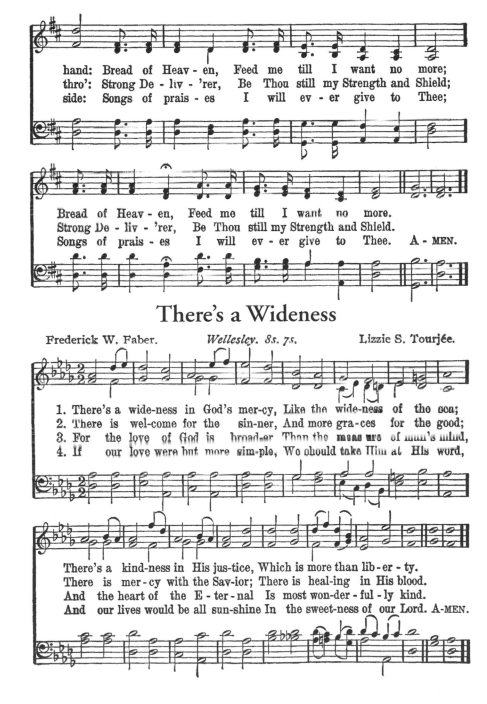

hand: Bread of Heav - en, Feed me till I want no more;
thro': Strong De - liv - 'rer, Be Thou still my Strength and Shield;
side: Songs of prais - es I will ev - er give to Thee;

Bread of Heav - en, Feed me till I want no more.
Strong De - liv - 'rer, Be Thou still my Strength and Shield.
Songs of prais - es I will ev - er give to Thee. A - MEN.

There's a Wideness

Frederick W. Faber. *Wellesley. 8s. 7s.* Lizzie S. Tourjée.

1. There's a wide-ness in God's mer-cy, Like the wide-ness of the sea;
2. There is wel-come for the sin-ner, And more gra-ces for the good;
3. For the love of God is broad-er Than the meas-ure of man's mind,
4. If our love were but more sim-ple, We should take Him at His word,

There's a kind-ness in His jus-tice, Which is more than lib - er - ty.
There is mer - cy with the Sav-ior; There is heal-ing in His blood.
And the heart of the E - ter-nal Is most won-der - ful - ly kind.
And our lives would be all sun-shine In the sweet-ness of our Lord. A-MEN.

Jesus Calls Us

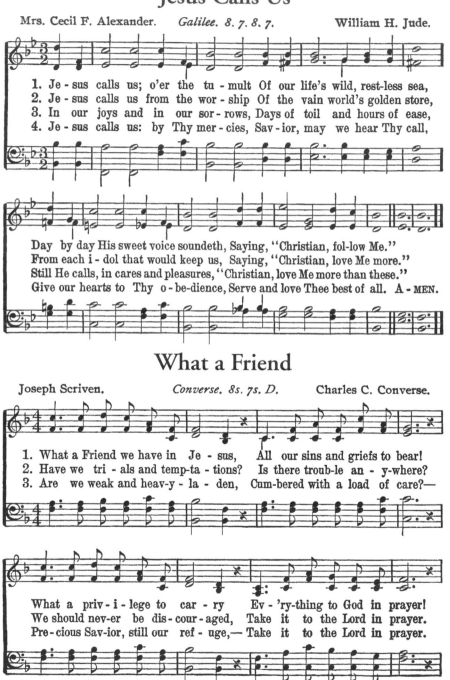

Mrs. Cecil F. Alexander.   *Galilee. 8. 7. 8. 7.*   William H. Jude.

1. Je - sus calls us; o'er the tu - mult Of our life's wild, rest-less sea,
2. Je - sus calls us from the wor - ship Of the vain world's golden store,
3. In our joys and in our sor - rows, Days of toil and hours of ease,
4. Je - sus calls us: by Thy mer - cies, Sav-ior, may we hear Thy call,

Day by day His sweet voice soundeth, Saying, "Christian, fol-low Me."
From each i - dol that would keep us, Saying, "Christian, love Me more."
Still He calls, in cares and pleasures, "Christian, love Me more than these."
Give our hearts to Thy o - be-dience, Serve and love Thee best of all. A - MEN.

What a Friend

Joseph Scriven.   *Converse. 8s. 7s. D.*   Charles C. Converse.

1. What a Friend we have in Je - sus,   All our sins and griefs to bear!
2. Have we tri - als and temp-ta - tions?   Is there troub-le an - y-where?
3. Are we weak and heav-y - la - den,   Cum-bered with a load of care?—

What a priv-i - lege to car - ry   Ev - 'ry-thing to God in prayer!
We should nev-er be dis-cour-aged,   Take it to the Lord in prayer.
Pre - cious Sav-ior, still our ref - uge,— Take it to the Lord in prayer.

What a Friend

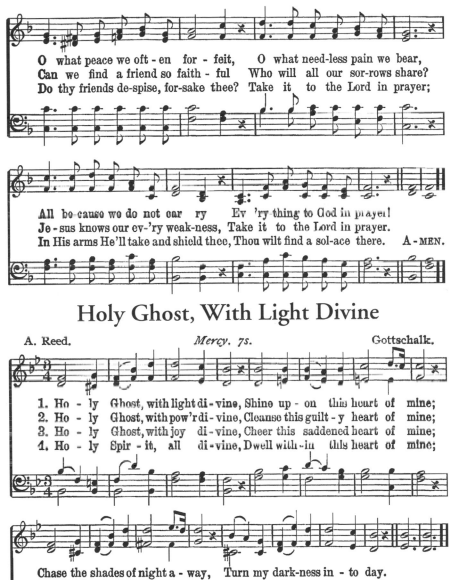

O what peace we oft-en for-feit, O what need-less pain we bear,
Can we find a friend so faith-ful Who will all our sor-rows share?
Do thy friends de-spise, for-sake thee? Take it to the Lord in prayer;

All be-cause we do not car-ry Ev-'ry-thing to God in prayer!
Je-sus knows our ev-'ry weak-ness, Take it to the Lord in prayer.
In His arms He'll take and shield thee, Thou wilt find a sol-ace there. A-MEN.

Holy Ghost, With Light Divine

A. Reed. Mercy. 7s. Gottschalk.

1. Ho-ly Ghost, with light di-vine, Shine up-on this heart of mine;
2. Ho-ly Ghost, with pow'r di-vine, Cleanse this guilt-y heart of mine;
3. Ho-ly Ghost, with joy di-vine, Cheer this saddened heart of mine;
4. Ho-ly Spir-it, all di-vine, Dwell with-in this heart of mine;

Chase the shades of night a-way, Turn my dark-ness in-to day.
Long hath sin with-out con-trol, Held do-min-ion o'er my soul.
Bid my man-y woes de-part, Heal my wounded, bleeding heart.
Cast down ev-'ry i-dol-throne, Reign supreme—and reign alone. A-MEN.

Jesus Shall Reign

Isaac Watts. *Duke Street. L. M.* John Hatton.

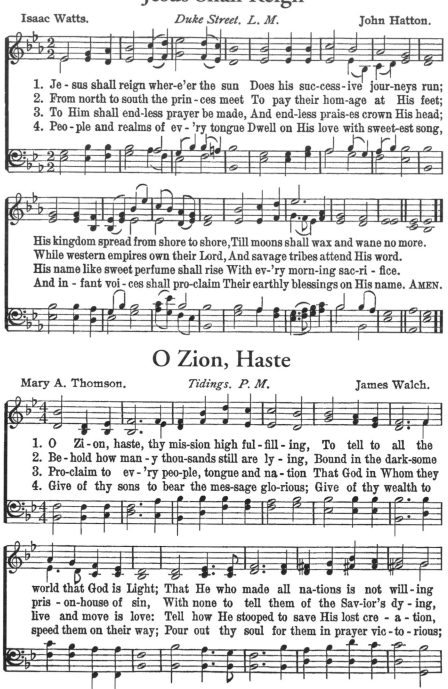

1. Je - sus shall reign wher-e'er the sun Does his suc-cess-ive jour-neys run;
2. From north to south the prin - ces meet To pay their hom-age at His feet;
3. To Him shall end-less prayer be made, And end-less prais-es crown His head;
4. Peo - ple and realms of ev - 'ry tongue Dwell on His love with sweet-est song,

His kingdom spread from shore to shore, Till moons shall wax and wane no more.
While western empires own their Lord, And savage tribes attend His word.
His name like sweet perfume shall rise With ev-'ry morn-ing sac-ri - fice.
And in - fant voi - ces shall pro-claim Their earthly blessings on His name. AMEN.

O Zion, Haste

Mary A. Thomson. *Tidings. P. M.* James Walch.

1. O Zi - on, haste, thy mis-sion high ful - fill - ing, To tell to all the
2. Be - hold how man - y thou-sands still are ly - ing, Bound in the dark-some
3. Pro-claim to ev - 'ry peo-ple, tongue and na - tion That God in Whom they
4. Give of thy sons to bear the mes-sage glo-rious; Give of thy wealth to

world that God is Light; That He who made all na-tions is not will-ing
pris - on-house of sin, With none to tell them of the Sav-ior's dy - ing,
live and move is love: Tell how He stooped to save His lost cre - a - tion,
speed them on their way; Pour out thy soul for them in prayer vic - to - rious;

Take Time to Be Holy

W. D. Longstaff.   COPYRIGHT, 1917. BY GEO. C. STEBBINS. RENEWAL.   George C. Stebbins.

1. Take time to be ho - ly, Speak oft with thy Lord; A - bide in Him
2. Take time to be ho - ly, The world rush-es on; Spend much time in
3. Take time to be ho - ly, Let Him be thy Guide; And run not be-
4. Take time to be ho - ly, Be calm in thy soul; Each tho't and each

al-ways, And feed on His Word. Make friends of God's children; Help those who are
se - cret With Je - sus a - lone— By look-ing to Je - sus, Like Him thou shalt
fore Him, What-ev-er be - tide; In joy or in sor - row, Still fol-low thy
mo - tive Be-neath His con-trol; Thus led by His Spir - it To foun-tains of

weak; For - get-ting in noth - ing His bless-ings to seek.
be; Thy friends in thy con - duct His like-ness shall see.
Lord, And, look-ing to Je - sus, Still trust in His Word.
love, Thou soon shalt be fit - ted For serv-ice a - bove.   A - MEN.

Be Ye Holy, For I Am Holy

As obedient children, not fashioning yourselves according to the former lusts in your ignorance:

But as he which hath called you is holy, so be ye holy in all manner of conversation;

Because it is written, Be ye holy; for I am holy.

1 Peter 1:14

My Soul, Be On Thy Guard

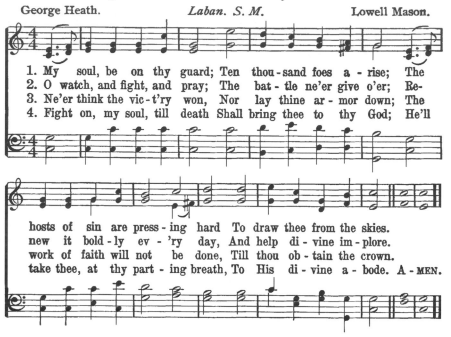

George Heath.   *Laban. S. M.*   Lowell Mason.

1. My soul, be on thy guard; Ten thou-sand foes a - rise; The hosts of sin are press-ing hard To draw thee from the skies.
2. O watch, and fight, and pray; The bat - tle ne'er give o'er; Re-new it bold-ly ev - 'ry day, And help di - vine im-plore.
3. Ne'er think the vic-t'ry won, Nor lay thine ar - mor down; The work of faith will not be done, Till thou ob - tain the crown.
4. Fight on, my soul, till death Shall bring thee to thy God; He'll take thee, at thy part - ing breath, To His di - vine a - bode. A - MEN.

Fairest Lord Jesus

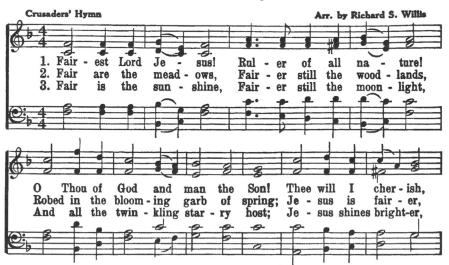

Crusaders' Hymn   Arr. by Richard S. Willis

1. Fair - est Lord Je - sus! Rul - er of all na - ture! O Thou of God and man the Son! Thee will I cher - ish,
2. Fair are the mead - ows, Fair - er still the wood - lands, Robed in the bloom-ing garb of spring; Je - sus is fair - er,
3. Fair is the sun - shine, Fair - er still the moon - light, And all the twin - kling star - ry host; Je - sus shines bright-er,

Fairest Lord Jesus

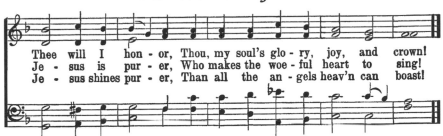

Thee will I hon - or, Thou, my soul's glo - ry, joy, and crown!
Je - sus is pur - er, Who makes the woe - ful heart to sing!
Je - sus shines pur - er, Than all the an - gels heav'n can boast!

Nearer, My God, to Thee

Sarah F. Adams.   Bethany. 6. 4.   Arr. by Lowell Mason.

1. Near - er, my God, to Thee, Near - er to Thee! E'en though it
2. Though like the wan - der - er, The sun gone down, Dark - ness be
3. There let the way ap - pear, Steps un - to Heav'n: All that Thou
4. Then, with my wak - ing tho'ts Bright with Thy praise, Out of my
5. Or if on joy - ful wing, Cleav - ing the sky, Sun, moon, and

be a cross That rais - eth me; Still all my song shall be, Near - er, my
o - ver me, My rest a stone, Yet in my dreams I'd be Near - er, my
send'st to me, In mer - cy giv'n: An - gels to beck - on me, Near - er, my
sto - ny griefs Beth - el I'll raise; So by my woes to be Near - er, my
stars for - got, Up - wards I fly, Still all my song shall be, Near - er, my

God, to Thee, Near - er, my God, to Thee, Near - er to Thee! A - MEN.

To the Harvest-field

C. H. G.

WORDS AND MUSIC COPYRIGHT, 1896, BY E. O. EXCELL. E. O. EXCELL, OWNER.

Chas. H. Gabriel.

Unison.

1. A band of faith-ful reap-ers we,   Who gath-er for e - ter - ni - ty
2. We are a faith-ful gleaning band,   And la-bor at our Lord's command,
3. The golden hours like moments fly,   And harvest days are pass-ing by;

The golden sheaves of ripened grain From ev'ry val - ley, hill and plain:
Un-yield-ing, loy-al, tried and true, For lo! the reap-ers are but few:
Then take thy rust-y sick - le down, And la - bor for a fade-less crown:

Our song is one the reap-ers sing,   In hon-or of the Lord and King—
Be-hold the wav-ing har-vest-field   A-bun-dant with a gold-en yield;
Why will you i - dly stand and wait?   Be-hold, the hour is grow-ing late!

To the Harvest-field

The Mas-ter of the harvest wide, Who for a world of sin-ners died.
And hear the Lord of harvest say To all, "Go reap for Me to - day."
Can you to judgment bring but leaves, While here are waiting golden sheaves?

CHORUS.

To the har-vest-field a-way, For the Mas-ter call-eth; There is work for

all to-day, Ere the dark-ness fall-eth. Swift-ly do the mo-ments fly,

Harvest days are going by, Go-ing, go-ing, go-ing, go-ing by. A-MEN.

Awake, My Soul, Stretch Every Nerve

CHRISTMAS C. M. with repeat

Philip Doddridge, 1755

George Frederick Handel, 1728

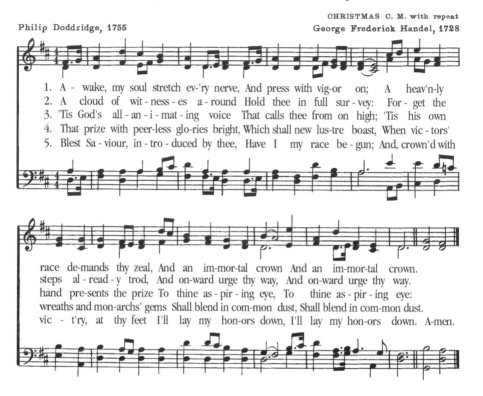

1. A - wake, my soul stretch ev-'ry nerve, And press with vig-or on; A heav'n-ly
2. A cloud of wit - ness - es a - round Hold thee in full sur - vey: For - get the
3. 'Tis God's all - an - i - mat - ing voice That calls thee from on high; 'Tis his own
4. That prize with peer-less glo-ries bright, Which shall new lus-tre boast, When vic - tors'
5. Blest Sa - viour, in - tro - duced by thee, Have I my race be - gun; And, crown'd with

race de-mands thy zeal, And an im-mor-tal crown And an im-mor-tal crown.
steps al - read - y trod, And on-ward urge thy way, And on-ward urge thy way.
hand pre-sents the prize To thine as - pir - ing eye, To thine as - pir - ing eye:
wreaths and mon-archs' gems Shall blend in com-mon dust, Shall blend in com-mon dust.
vic - t'ry, at thy feet I'll lay my hon-ors down, I'll lay my hon-ors down. A-men.

Let Us Run the Heavenly Race

Wherefore seeing we also are compassed about with so great a cloud of witnesses, let us lay aside every weight, and the sin which doth so easily beset us, and let us run with patience the race that is set before us,

Looking unto Jesus the author and finisher of our faith; who for the joy that was set before him endured the cross, despising the shame, and is set down at the right hand of the throne of God.

For consider him that endured such contradiction of sinners against himself, lest ye be wearied and faint in your minds.

Hebrews 12:1–3

Blessed Assurance

Fanny J. Crosby.

Mrs. J. F. Knapp.

1. Bless-ed as-sur-ance, Je-sus is mine! Oh, what a fore-taste of
2. Per-fect sub-mis-sion, per-fect de-light, Vi-sions of rap-ture now
3. Per-fect sub-mis-sion, all is at rest, I in my Sav-ior am

glo-ry di-vine! Heir of sal-va-tion, pur-chase of God,
burst on my sight; An-gels de-scend-ing, bring from a-bove
hap-py and blest; Watch-ing and wait-ing, look-ing a-bove,

CHORUS.

Born of His Spir-it, washed in His blood.
Ech-oes of mer-cy, whis-pers of love. This is my sto-ry, this is my
Filled with His goodness, lost in His love.

song, Prais-ing my Sav-ior all the day long; This is my sto-ry,

this is my song, Prais-ing my Sav-ior all the day long. A-MEN.

Yield Not to Temptation

H. R. P.   COPYRIGHT, 1897, BY H. R. PALMER. RENEWAL.   H. R. Palmer.

1. Yield not to temp-ta-tion, For yield-ing is sin; Each vic-t'ry will
2. Shun e-vil com-pan-ions, Bad language dis-dain, God's name hold in
3. To him that o'er-com-eth God giv-eth a crown, Thro' faith we shall

help you Some oth-er to win; Fight man-ful-ly on-ward,
rev-'rence, Nor take it in vain; Be thought-ful and ear-nest,
con-quer, Tho' oft-en cast down; He who is our Sav-ior,

Dark pas-sions sub-due, Look ev-er to Je-sus, He'll car-ry you through.
Kind-heart-ed and true, Look ev-er to Je-sus, He'll car-ry you through.
Our strength will re-new, Look ev-er to Je-sus, He'll car-ry you through.

CHORUS.

Ask the Sav-ior to help you, Com-fort, strengthen and keep you;

He is will-ing to aid you, He will car-ry you through. A-MEN.

Savior, Like a Shepherd Lead Us

Anonymous.   *Shepherd.* 8. 7. 8. 7. 4. 7.   William B. Bradbury.

1. Sav - ior, like a shep-herd lead us,   Much we need Thy ten-der care;
2. We are Thine; do Thou be-friend us,   Be the Guard-ian of our way;
3. Thou hast prom-ised to re - ceive us, Poor and sin-ful though we be;
4. Ear - ly let us seek Thy fa - vor; Ear - ly let us do Thy will;

In   Thy pleas-ant pas-tures feed us,   For our use Thy folds pre-pare:
Keep Thy flock, from sin de - fend us,   Seek us when we go a - stray:
Thou hast mer-cy to   re - lieve us,   Grace to cleanse, and pow'r to free:
Bless-ed Lord and on - ly Sav - ior, With Thy love our bos-oms fill:

Bless-ed Je-sus, Bless-ed Je-sus, Thou hast bought us, Thine we are; Blessed
Bless-ed Je-sus, Bless-ed Je-sus, Hear the children when they pray; Blessed
Bless-ed Je-sus, Bless-ed Je-sus, Ear - ly let us turn to Thee, Blessed
Bless-ed Je-sus, Bless-ed Je-sus, Thou hast loved us, love us still;   Blessed

Je - sus, Bless-ed Je - sus, Thou hast bought us, Thine we are.
Je - sus, Bless-ed Je - sus, Hear the chil-dren when they pray.
Je - sus, Bless-ed Je - sus, Ear - ly let us turn to Thee.
Je - sus, Bless-ed Je - sus, Thou hast loved us, love us still.   A - MEN.

Break Thou the Bread of Life

Mary Ann Lathbury.　*Bread of Life. 6. 4. D.*　William F. Sherwin.

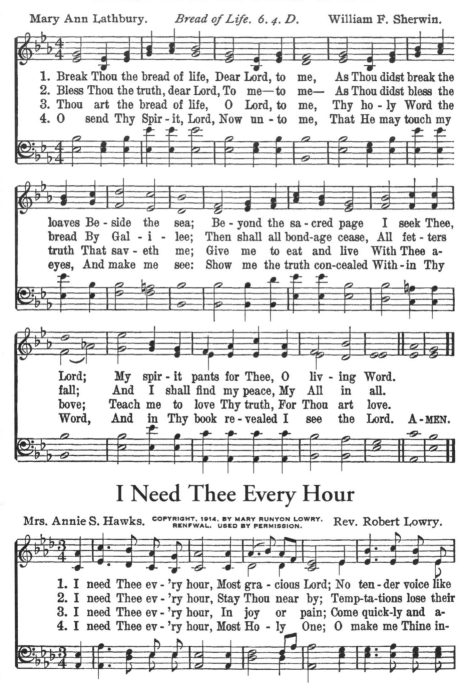

1. Break Thou the bread of life, Dear Lord, to me, As Thou didst break the
2. Bless Thou the truth, dear Lord, To me—to me— As Thou didst bless the
3. Thou art the bread of life, O Lord, to me, Thy ho - ly Word the
4. O send Thy Spir - it, Lord, Now un - to me, That He may touch my

loaves Be - side the sea; Be - yond the sa - cred page I seek Thee,
bread By Gal - i - lee; Then shall all bond-age cease, All fet - ters
truth That sav - eth me; Give me to eat and live With Thee a -
eyes, And make me see: Show me the truth con-cealed With-in Thy

Lord; My spir - it pants for Thee, O liv - ing Word.
fall; And I shall find my peace, My All in all.
bove; Teach me to love Thy truth, For Thou art love.
Word, And in Thy book re - vealed I see the Lord. A - MEN.

I Need Thee Every Hour

Mrs. Annie S. Hawks.　　Rev. Robert Lowry.

1. I need Thee ev - 'ry hour, Most gra - cious Lord; No ten - der voice like
2. I need Thee ev - 'ry hour, Stay Thou near by; Temp-ta-tions lose their
3. I need Thee ev - 'ry hour, In joy or pain; Come quick-ly and a -
4. I need Thee ev - 'ry hour, Most Ho - ly One; O make me Thine in -

I Need Thee Every Hour

CHORUS.

Thine Can peace af - ford.
pow'r When Thou art nigh.   I need Thee, O, I need Thee; Ev - 'ry hour I
bide, Or life is vain.
deed, Thou bless - ed Son.

need Thee! O bless me now, my Sav - ior, I come to Thee! A - MEN.

Now the Day is Over

Sabine Baring-Gould.   *Barnby. 6s. 5s.*   Joseph Barnby.

1. Now the day is o - ver,   Night is draw - ing nigh,
2. Je - sus, give the wear - y   Calm and sweet re - pose;
3. Grant to lit - tle chil - dren   Vi - sions bright of Thee;
4. Thro' the long night-watch-es,   May Thine an - gels spread
5. When the morn - ing wak - ens,   Then may I a - rise,

Shad - ows of the eve - ning   Steal a - cross the sky.
With Thy ten-d'rest bless - ing   May our eye - lids close.
Guard the sail - ors toss - ing   On the deep blue sea.
Their white wings a - bove me,   Watch-ing round my bed.
Pure and fresh and sin - less   In Thy ho - ly eyes. A - MEN.

Steal a - cross   the sky.

Come, Sound His Praise

Isaac Watts.　　　*Silver Street. S. M.*　　　Isaac Smith.

1. Come, sound His praise a - broad, And hymns of glo - ry sing; Je-
2. He formed the deeps un-known; He gave the seas their bound; The
3. Come, wor - ship at His throne, Come, bow be - fore the Lord; We
4. To - day at - tend His voice, Nor dare pro - voke His rod; Come,

ho - vah is the sov - 'reign God, The u - ni - ver - sal King.
wa - t'ry worlds are all His own, And all the sol - id ground.
are His works, and not our own; He formed us by His word.
like the peo - ple of His choice, And own your gra-cious God. A-MEN.

Angel Voices, Ever Singing

Francis Pott.　　*Angel Voices. 8. 5. 8. 5. 8. 4. 3.*　　Sir Arthur Sullivan.

1. An - gel voi - ces, ev - er sing - ing Round Thy throne of light,
2. Thou who art be - yond the far - thest Mor - tal eye can scan,
3. Here, great God, to - day we of - fer Of Thine own to Thee;
4. Hon - or, glo - ry, might, and mer - it, Thine shall ev - er be,

An - gel harps, for-ev - er ring - ing, Rest not day nor night; Thou-sands
Can it be that Thou re-gard - est Songs of sin - ful man? Can we
And for Thine ac-cept-ance prof-fer, All un - wor - thi - ly, Hearts and
Fa - ther, Son, and Ho - ly Spir - it, Bless-ed Trin - i - ty: Of the

Angel Voices, Ever Singing

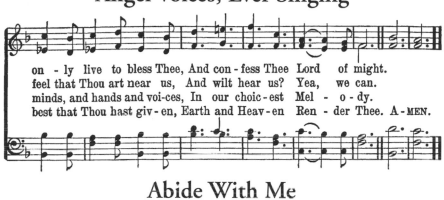

on - ly live to bless Thee, And con - fess Thee Lord of might.
feel that Thou art near us, And wilt hear us? Yea, we can.
minds, and hands and voi - ces, In our choic - est Mel - o - dy.
best that Thou hast giv - en, Earth and Heav - en Ren - der Thee. A - MEN.

Abide With Me

H. F. Lyte.   *Eventide. 10s.*   W. H. Monk.

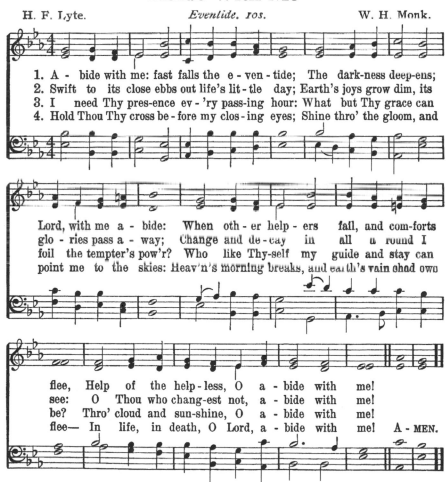

1. A - bide with me: fast falls the e - ven - tide; The dark-ness deep-ens;
2. Swift to its close ebbs out life's lit - tle day; Earth's joys grow dim, its
3. I need Thy pres-ence ev - 'ry pass-ing hour: What but Thy grace can
4. Hold Thou Thy cross be - fore my clos - ing eyes; Shine thro' the gloom, and

Lord, with me a - bide: When oth - er help - ers fail, and com-forts
glo - ries pass a - way; Change and de-cay in all a round I
foil the tempter's pow'r? Who like Thy-self my guide and stay can
point me to the skies: Heav'n's morning breaks, and earth's vain shad ow

flee, Help of the help - less, O a - bide with me!
see: O Thou who chang-est not, a - bide with me!
be? Thro' cloud and sun-shine, O a - bide with me!
flee— In life, in death, O Lord, a - bide with me! A - MEN.

Little Sunbeams

Eben E. Rexford.

Chas. H. Gabriel.

1. I think God gives the children, As thro' the land they go, The most de-light-ful mis-sion That an-y one can know; He wants us to be sun-beams Of love and hope and cheer, To brighten up the shadows That oft-en gath-er here.

2. The clouds may hide the sunshine Of Heaven from our sight, And life have much of sor-row To mar the heart's de-light; But if like faith-ful sun-beams, We chil-dren do our part, We'll bring a ray of brightness To ev-'ry shadowed heart.

3. Then let us live our mis-sion Of sunbeams day by day, And scatter joy and bright-ness A-bout us all the way; Let's chase a-way life's shad-ows With lov-ing tho't and deed, And be the sunshine-makers, Of which the world has need.

Chorus.

O we are lit-tle sun-beams, Sent down from God to man; In all life's sha-dy pla-ces We shine as best we can. A-MEN.

I'll Be a Sunbeam

Nellie Talbot.

E. O. Excell.

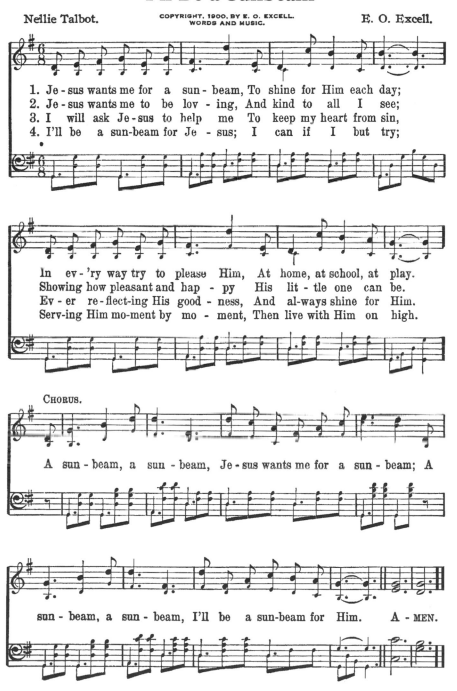

1. Je-sus wants me for a sun-beam, To shine for Him each day;
2. Je-sus wants me to be lov-ing, And kind to all I see;
3. I will ask Je-sus to help me To keep my heart from sin,
4. I'll be a sun-beam for Je-sus; I can if I but try;

In ev-'ry way try to please Him, At home, at school, at play.
Showing how pleasant and hap-py His lit-tle one can be.
Ev-er re-flect-ing His good-ness, And al-ways shine for Him.
Serv-ing Him mo-ment by mo-ment, Then live with Him on high.

CHORUS.

A sun-beam, a sun-beam, Je-sus wants me for a sun-beam; A

sun-beam, a sun-beam, I'll be a sun-beam for Him. A-MEN.

Bring Them In

Alexcenah Thomas.

COPYRIGHT PROPERTY OF MRS. W. A. OGDEN.
USED BY PERMISSION.

W. A. Ogden.

1. Hark! 'tis the Shepherd's voice I hear, Out in the des-ert dark and drear,
2. Who'll go and help this Shepherd kind, Help Him the wand'ring ones to find?
3. Out in the des-ert hear their cry, Out on the mountains wild and high;

Call-ing the sheep who've gone astray Far from the Shepherd's fold a - way.
Who'll bring the lost ones to the fold, Where they'll be sheltered from the cold?
Hark! 'tis the Mas-ter speaks to thee, "Go find My sheep wher-e'er they be."

CHORUS.

Bring them in, bring them in, Bring them in from the fields of sin;

Bring them in, bring them in, Bring the wand'ring ones to Je-sus.   A-MEN.

His Holy Temple

E. O. E.

The Lord is in His ho - ly tem - ple, Let all the

His Holy Temple

earth keep si - lence, keep si - lence be - fore .. Him. A-MEN.

Dear Little Stranger

C. H. G.

Chas. H. Gabriel.

1. Low in a man - ger—dear lit - tle Stran - ger, Je - sus, the won-der-ful
2. An - gels de-scend-ing, o - ver Him bend - ing, Chant-ed a ten-der and
3. Dear lit - tle Stran-ger, born in a man - ger, Mak-er and Monarch, and

Sav-ior, was born; There was none to receive Him, none to believe Him, None but the
si - lent re-frain; Then a won-der-ful sto - ry told of His glo - ry, Un-to the
Sav-ior of all; I will love Thee for-ev-er! grieve Thee? no, never! Thou didst for

CHORUS.

an-gels were watching that morn. { Dear lit - tle Stranger, slept in a man - ger,
shepherd's on Bethlehem's plain. { But with the poor He slumbered se-cure, The
me make Thy bed in a stall.

1   2

No down-y pil - low un - der His head; dear lit-tle Babe in His bed.   A-MEN.

That Sweet Story of Old

Mrs. Jemima Luke.　　　　　*Davenant. 11s. 8s. D.*　　　　　Old Melody.

1. I think when I read that sweet sto - ry of old, When
2. Yet still to His foot - stool in prayer I may go, And

Je - sus was here a - mong men, How He called lit - tle chil - dren as
ask for a share in His love; And if I now ear - nest - ly

lambs to His fold, I should like to have been with them then.
seek Him be - low, I shall see Him and hear Him a - bove.

I wish that His hands had been placed on my head, That His
In that beau - ti - ful home He has gone to pre - pare For

arms had been thrown a - round me, And that I might have seen His kind
all who are washed and for - giv'n; And man - y dear chil - dren are

That Sweet Story of Old

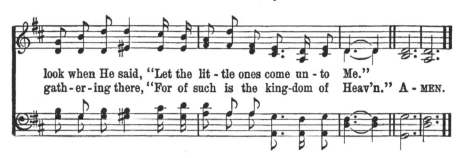

look when He said, "Let the lit-tle ones come un-to Me."
gath-er-ing there, "For of such is the king-dom of Heav'n." A-MEN.

Jesus Bids Us Shine

COPYRIGHT, 1912, BY E. O. EXCELL. RENEWAL.
E. O. Excell.

1. Je-sus bids us shine, With a clear, pure light, Like a lit-tle
2. Je-sus bids us shine, First of all for Him; Well He sees and
3. Je-sus bids us shine, Then, for all a-round Man-y kinds of
4. Je-sus bids us shine, As we work for Him, Bring-ing those that

can-dle Burn-ing in the night; In this world of dark-ness
knows it If our light is dim; He looks down from Heav-en,
dark-ness In this world a-bound— Sin and want and sor-row;
wan-der From the paths of sin; He will ev-er help us,

We must shine, You in your small cor-ner, And I in mine.
Sees us shine, You in your small cor-ner, And I in mine.
We must shine, You in your small cor-ner, And I in mine.
If we shine, You in your small cor-ner, And I in mine. A-MEN.

Mighty Army of the Young

John R. Colgan.   A. F. Myers.

1. Might - y ar - my of the young, Lift the voice in cheer - ful song,
2. Tongues of chil-dren light and free, Tongues of youth all full of glee,
3. Je - sus lives, O bless - ed words! King of kings, and Lord of lords!

Send the wel-come word a - long, Je - sus lives! Once He died for you and me,
Sing to all on land and sea, Je - sus lives! Light for you and all man-kind,
Lift the cross and sheathe the swords, Je - sus lives! See, He breaks the prison wall,

Bore our sins up - on the tree, Now He lives to make us free,   Je - sus lives!
Sight for all by sin made blind, Life in Je - sus all may find,   Je - sus lives!
Throws a - side the dreadful pall, Conquers death at once for all,   Je - sus lives!

CHORUS.

Wait not till the shad-ows lengthen, till you old - er grow, Ral - ly now and
Wait   not   Sing,
Wait   not,   wait   not,   Sing   for

sing for Je - sus, ev - 'ry-where you go; Lift your joy - ful voi - ces high,
sing,
Je - sus,

Mighty Army of the Young

Ringing clear thro' earth and sky, Let the blessed tidings fly, Je-sus lives! A-MEN.

Wonderful Words of Life

P. P. B.

COPYRIGHT, 1917, BY THE JOHN CHURCH CO.
USED BY PERMISSION.

P. P. Bliss.

1. Sing them o-ver a-gain to me, Won-der-ful words of Life;
2. Christ, the bless-ed One, gives to all, Won-der-ful words of Life;
3. Sweet-ly ech-o the gos-pel call, Won-der-ful words of Life;

Let me more of their beau-ty see, Won-der-ful words of Life.
Sin-ner, list to the lov-ing call, Won-der-ful words of Life.
Of-fer par-don and peace to all, Won-der-ful words of Life.

Words of life and beau-ty, Teach me faith and du-ty:
All so free-ly giv-en, Woo-ing us to Heav-en:
Je-sus, on-ly Sav-ior, Sanc-ti-fy for-ev-er:

REFRAIN.

Beau-ti-ful words, wonderful words, Wonderful words of Life. Life. A-MEN.

Precious Word

C. H. G.

COPYRIGHT, 1904, BY CHAS. H. GABRIEL.
E. O. EXCELL, OWNER.

Chas. H. Gabriel.

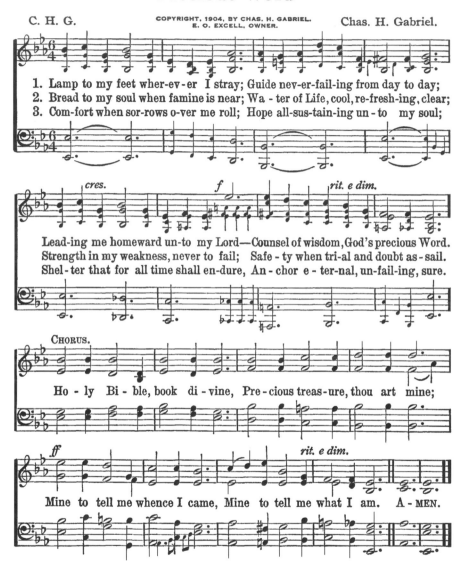

1. Lamp to my feet wher-ev-er I stray; Guide nev-er-fail-ing from day to day;
2. Bread to my soul when famine is near; Wa - ter of Life, cool, re-fresh-ing, clear;
3. Com-fort when sor-rows o-ver me roll; Hope all-sus-tain-ing un-to my soul;

Lead-ing me homeward un-to my Lord—Counsel of wisdom, God's precious Word.
Strength in my weakness, never to fail; Safe - ty when tri-al and doubt as-sail.
Shel - ter that for all time shall en-dure, An - chor e-ter-nal, un-fail-ing, sure.

CHORUS.

Ho - ly Bi - ble, book di - vine, Pre - cious treas-ure, thou art mine;

Mine to tell me whence I came, Mine to tell me what I am. A - MEN.

Of the Holy Scripture

The whole counsel of God concerning all things necessary for His own glory, man's salvation, faith and life, is either expressly set down in Scripture, or by good and necessary consequence may be deduced from Scripture.... WCF 1.6

America the Beautiful

Katherine Lee Bates.   *Materna. C. M. D.*   Samuel A. Ward.

1. O beau - ti - ful for spa-cious skies, For am - ber waves of grain,
2. O beau - ti - ful for pil-grim feet, Whose stern, im-pas-sioned stress
3. O beau - ti - ful for he - roes proved In lib - er - at - ing strife,
4. O beau - ti - ful for pa-triot dream That sees be-yond the years

For pur - ple moun-tain maj - es - ties A - bove the fruit-ed plain!
A thor-ough-fare for free-dom beat A - cross the wil - der - ness!
Who more than self their coun-try loved, And mer - cy more than life!
Thine al - a - bas - ter cit - ies gleam, Undimmed by hu - man tears!

A - mer - i - ca! A - mer - i - ca! God shed His grace on thee,
A - mer - i - ca! A - mer - i - ca! God mend thine ev - 'ry flaw,
A - mer - i - ca! A - mer - i - ca! May God thy gold re - fine,
A - mer - i - ca! A - mer - i - ca! God shed His grace on thee,

And crown thy good with broth-er-hood From sea to shin-ing sea!
Con - firm thy soul in self - con-trol, Thy lib-er-ty in law!
Till all suc-cess be no - ble-ness, And ev-'ry gain di - vine!
And crown thy good with broth-er-hood From sea to shin-ing sea!   A-MEN.

The Red, White, and Blue

1. O Co-lum-bia! the gem of the o-cean, The home of the brave and the free;
2. When war winged its wide des-o-la-tion, And threatened the land to de-form,
3. Then, sons of Co-lum-bia! come hith-er, And join in our nation's sweet hymn;

The shrine of each patriot's devotion,   A world of-fers hom-age to thee.
The ark then of freedom's foundation,   Co - lum-bia rode safe thro' the storm;
May the wreaths they have won never wither, Nor the stars of their glory grow dim!

Thy mandates make heroes assemble,   When Liberty's form stands in view;
With her garlands of vict'ry around her, When so proudly she bore her brave crew,
May the serv-ice, u-nit-ed, ne'er sev-er,   But they to their col-ors prove true!

Thy ban-ners make tyr-an-ny trem-ble, When borne by the red, white and blue.
With her flag proudly waving before her, The boast of the red, white and blue.
The   Ar - my and Na-vy for-ev-er, Three cheers for the red, white and blue.

REFRAIN.

When borne by the red, white and blue, When borne by the red, white and blue; Thy
The   boast of the red, white and blue, The boast of the red, white and blue; With her
Three cheers for the red, white and blue, Three cheers for the red, white and blue; The

The Red, White, and Blue

banners make tyr-an-ny tremble, When borne by the red, white and blue.
flag proudly waving be-fore her, The boast of the red, white and blue.
Ar-my and Na-vy for-ev-er, Three cheers for the red, white and blue. A-MEN.

My Country 'Tis of Thee

S. F. Smith.   *America.*   English.

1. My coun-try, 'tis of thee, Sweet land of lib-er-ty,
2. My na-tive coun-try, thee, Land of the no-ble, free,
3. Let mu-sic swell the breeze, And ring from all the trees
4. Our fa-ther's God! to Thee, Au-thor of lib-er-ty,

Of thee I sing: Land where my fa-thers died, Land of the
Thy name I love: I love thy rocks and rills, Thy woods and
Sweet free-dom's song: Let mor-tal tongues a-wake; Let all that
To Thee we sing: Long may our land be bright With free-dom's

pil-grim's pride, From ev-'ry moun-tain-side Let free-dom ring!
tem-pled hills; My heart with rap-ture thrills Like that a-bove.
breathe partake, Let rocks their si-lence break, The sound pro-long.
ho-ly light; Pro-tect us by Thy might, Great God, our King! A-MEN.

This Is My Father's World

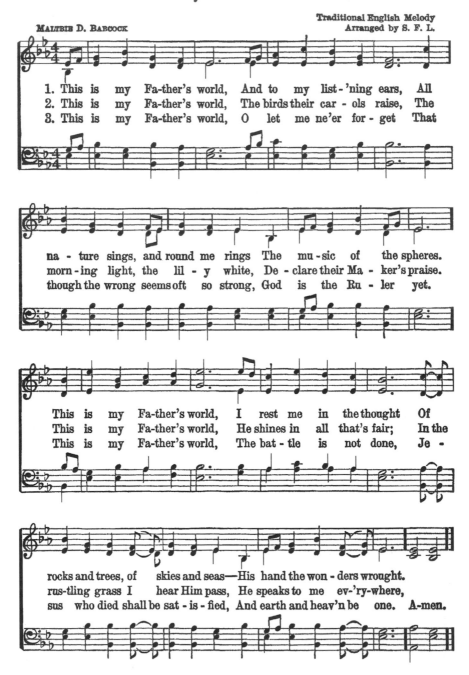

MALTBIE D. BABCOCK

Traditional English Melody
Arranged by S. F. L.

1. This is my Fa-ther's world, And to my list-'ning ears, All
2. This is my Fa-ther's world, The birds their car - ols raise, The
3. This is my Fa-ther's world, O let me ne'er for - get That

na - ture sings, and round me rings The mu - sic of the spheres.
morn - ing light, the lil - y white, De - clare their Ma - ker's praise.
though the wrong seems oft so strong, God is the Ru - ler yet.

This is my Fa-ther's world, I rest me in the thought Of
This is my Fa-ther's world, He shines in all that's fair; In the
This is my Fa-ther's world, The bat - tle is not done, Je -

rocks and trees, of skies and seas—His hand the won - ders wrought.
rus-tling grass I hear Him pass, He speaks to me ev-'ry-where.
sus who died shall be sat - is - fied, And earth and heav'n be one. A-men.

Redeemed

Fanny J. Crosby.

Wm. J. Kirkpatrick.

1. Redeemed—how I love to pro-claim it! Redeemed by the blood of the Lamb;
2. Redeemed and so happy in Je - sus, No language my rap-ture can tell;
3. I think of my bless-ed Re-deem-er, I think of Him all the day long;
4. I know I shall see in His beau-ty The King in whose law I de - light;

Redeemed thro' His in - fi-nite mer - cy, His child, and for - ev - er, I am.
I know that the light of His presence With me doth con-tin-ual - ly dwell.
I sing, for I can-not be si - lent; His love is the theme of my song.
Who lov - ing - ly guardeth my footsteps, And giv-eth me songs in the night.

CHORUS

Re - deemed, .. re - deemed, .. Redeemed by the blood of the Lamb;
re-deemed, re-deemed,

Re - deemed, .. re - deemed, .. His child, and for - ev - er, I am.
re-deemed, re-deemed,

The Star-Spangled Banner

Francis Scott Key.

1. Oh,   say, can you see, by the dawn's ear-ly light, What so proud-ly we
2. On the shore, dimly seen thro' the mists of the deep, Where the foe's haughty
3. And where is that band, who so vaunt-ing-ly swore That the hav - oc of
4. Oh, thus be it ev - er when freemen shall stand Be - tween their loved

hailed at the twilight's last gleaming? Whose broad stripes and bright stars, thro' the
host   in dread si-lence re - pos - es, What is that which the breeze, o'er the
war   and the bat-tle's con - fu - sion, A   home and a coun-try should
homes and the war's des - o - la - tion; Blest with vic - t'ry and peace, may the

per - il - ous fight, O'er the ramparts we watched, were so gallantly streaming?
tow - er - ing steep, As it fit - ful - ly blows, half conceals, half dis-clos - es?
leave us no more? Their blood has washed out their foul footsteps' pol-lu-tion;
Heav'n-rescued land Praise the Pow'r that hath made and preserved us a na-tion!

And the rock-ets' red glare, the bombs bursting in air, Gave proof thro' the
Now it catch-es the gleam of the morning's first beam, In full glo - ry re -
No   ref-uge could save the   hire-ling and slave From the ter - ror of
Then con-quer we must, when our cause it is just; And   this be our

The Star-Spangled Banner

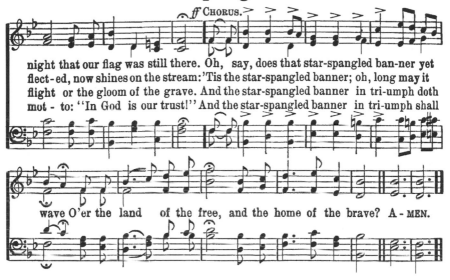

night that our flag was still there. Oh, say, does that star-spangled ban-ner yet
flect-ed, now shines on the stream: 'Tis the star-spangled banner; oh, long may it
flight or the gloom of the grave. And the star-spangled banner in tri-umph doth
mot - to: "In God is our trust!" And the star-spangled banner in tri-umph shall

wave O'er the land   of the free, and the home of the brave? A - MEN.

When I Survey the Wondrous Cross

ISAAC WATTS   HAMBURG. L. M.   Arr. by LOWELL MASON

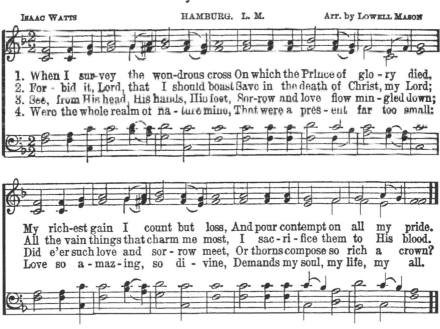

1. When I sur-vey the won-drous cross On which the Prince of glo - ry died,
2. For - bid it, Lord, that I should boast Save in the death of Christ, my Lord;
3. See, from His head, His hands, His feet, Sor-row and love flow min - gled down;
4. Were the whole realm of na - ture mine, That were a pres-ent far too small:

My rich-est gain I count but loss, And pour contempt on all my pride.
All the vain things that charm me most, I sac - ri - fice them to His blood.
Did e'er such love and sor - row meet, Or thorns compose so rich a crown?
Love so a-maz-ing, so di - vine, Demands my soul, my life, my all.

Loyal and True

Miss A. M. Goodman.   COPYRIGHT, 1892, BY W. A. GOODMAN,   H. W. Fairbank.
USED BY PERMISSION.

Voices in Unison.

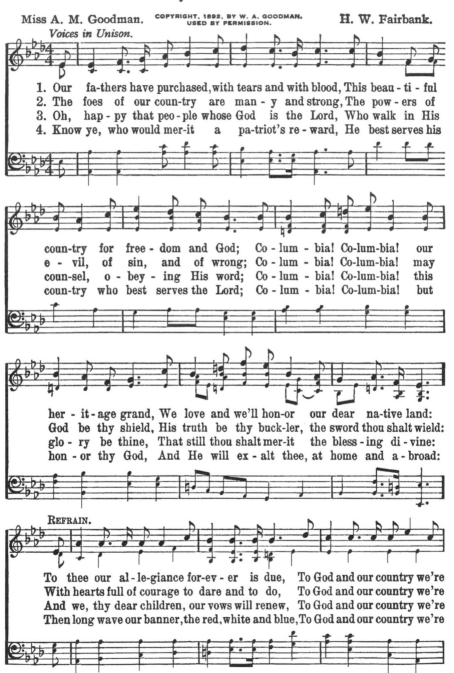

1. Our fa-thers have purchased, with tears and with blood, This beau-ti-ful
2. The foes of our coun-try are man-y and strong, The pow-ers of
3. Oh, hap-py that peo-ple whose God is the Lord, Who walk in His
4. Know ye, who would mer-it a pa-triot's re-ward, He best serves his

coun-try for free-dom and God; Co-lum-bia! Co-lum-bia! our
e-vil, of sin, and of wrong; Co-lum-bia! Co-lum-bia! may
coun-sel, o-bey-ing His word; Co-lum-bia! Co-lum-bia! this
coun-try who best serves the Lord; Co-lum-bia! Co-lum-bia! but

her-it-age grand, We love and we'll hon-or our dear na-tive land:
God be thy shield, His truth be thy buck-ler, the sword thou shalt wield:
glo-ry be thine, That still thou shalt mer-it the bless-ing di-vine:
hon-or thy God, And He will ex-alt thee, at home and a-broad:

REFRAIN.

To thee our al-le-giance for-ev-er is due, To God and our country we're
With hearts full of courage to dare and to do, To God and our country we're
And we, thy dear children, our vows will renew, To God and our country we're
Then long wave our banner, the red, white and blue, To God and our country we're

Loyal and True

loy - al and true; To thee our al - le-giance for - ev - er is due, To
loy - al and true; With hearts full of cour-age to dare and to do, To
loy - al and true; And we, thy dear children, our vows will re-new, To
loy - al and true; Then long wave our ban-ner, the red, white and blue, To

God and our coun-try we're loy - al and true. A-MEN.

God of Our Fathers

Rudyard Kipling. *St. Catherine. L. M. 6 l.* H. F. Hemy.

1. God of our fa-thers, known of old, Lord of our far-flung bat - tle-line,
2. The tu-mult and the shouting dies, The captains and the kings de - part;
3. Far-called, our na-vies melt a - way, On dune and headland sinks the fire;

Be-neath whose aw-ful hand we hold Do-min-ion o - ver palm and pine:
Still stands Thine ancient sac - ri - fice, An humble and a con - trite heart.
Lo, all our pomp of yes - ter-day Is one with Nin-e - veh and Tyre!

Lord God of Hosts, be with us yet, Lest we forget, lest we for-get! A-MEN.

Speed Our Republic

M. Keller.

1. Speed our Re-pub-lic, O Fa-ther on high, Lead us in
2. Fore-most in bat-tle, for Free-dom to stand, We rush to
3. Rise up, proud ea-gle, rise up to the clouds, Spread thy broad

path-ways of jus-tice and right; Ru-lers as well as the
arms when a-roused by its call; Still as of yore when George
wing o'er this fair west-ern world! Fling from thy beak our dear

ruled, one and all, Gir-dle with vir-tue, the ar-mor of might!
Wash-ing-ton led, Thunders our war-cry, "We con-quer or fall!"
ban-ner of old! Show that it still is for free-dom un-furled!

Hail! three times hail to our coun-try and flag! A-MEN.

Of the Civil Magistrate

God, the supreme Lord and King of all the world, hath ordained civil magistrates, to be, under Him, over the people, for His own glory, and the public good: and, to this end, hath armed them with power of the sword, for the defence and encouragement of them that are good, and for the punishment of evil doers.　　WCF 5.1

A Mighty Fortress

Maestoso.   Old Chorale.

1. A might-y for-tress is our God, A bul-wark nev-er fail-ing;
2. Did we in our own strength con-fide, Our striv-ing would be los-ing,
3. And though this world, with dev-ils filled, Should threaten to un-do us,
4. That word a-bove all earth-ly pow'rs—No thanks to them—a-bid-eth;

Our help-er He, a-mid the flood Of mor-tal ills pre-vail-ing.
Were not the right man on our side, The man of God's own choos-ing.
We will not fear, for God hath willed His truth to tri-umph through us.
The Spir-it and the gifts are ours Thro' Him who with us sid-eth;

For still our an-cient foe Doth seek to work us woe; His craft and pow'r are
Dost ask who that may be? Christ Je-sus, it is He; Lord Sab-aoth is His
The prince of dark-ness grim, We trem-ble not for him; His rage we can en-
Let goods and kin-dred go, This mor-tal life al-so; The bod-y they may

great, And, armed with cru-el hate, On earth is not his e-qual.
name, From age to age the same, And He must win the bat-tle.
dure, For lo! his doom is sure: One lit-tle word shall fell him.
kill; God's truth a-bid-eth still, His king-dom is for ev-er.

Awakening Chorus

Charlotte G. Homer.

Chas. H. Gabriel.

1. A - wake!   a - wake!   and sing the bless-ed sto - ry; A
A - wake!   a - wake!

2. Ring out!   ring out!   O bells of joy and glad-ness! Re-
Ring out!   ring out!

wake!   a - wake!   and let your song of praise a-rise; A-wake!   a-
A-wake!   a-wake!   A-wake!

peat,   re - peat   a - new the sto-ry o'er a-gain, Till all   the
Re-peat,   re-peat,   Till all

wake!   the earth is full of glo-ry, And light   is beam - ing
a-wake!   And light   is beam-ing

earth   shall lose its weight of sad-ness, And shout   a - new   the
the earth,   And shout   a-new

MALE VOICES IN UNISON.

from the ra-diant skies; The rocks and rills, the vales   and hills re-sound with
glo - ri - ous re-frain; With an-gels in   the heights sing of the great sal-

FULL HARMONY.

glad - ness, All na - ture joins   to sing the triumph song. The Lord Je-
va - tion He wrest - ed from   the hand of sin and death.

Awakening Chorus

All Hail, Immanuel

D. R. Van Sickle.

Chas. H. Gabriel.

1. All hail to Thee, Im-man-u-el, We cast . . . our crowns be-fore Thee;
2. All hail to Thee, Im-man-u-el, The ran - somed hosts surround Thee;
3. All hail to Thee, Im-man-u-el, Our ris - - en King and Sav-ior!

Let ev-'ry heart o - bey Thy will, And ev - - - 'ry voice a-
And earth-ly mon-archs clam-or forth Their Sov - - 'reign King to
Thy foes are van-quished, and Thou art Om - nip - - o - tent for-

dore Thee. In praise to Thee, our Sav - ior King, The vi - brant
crown Thee. While those re-deemed in a - ges gone, As - sem - bled
ev - er. Death, sin and hell no lon - ger reign, And Sa - tan's

chords of Heav - en ring, And ech - o back the might-y strain:
round the great white throne, Break forth in - to im - mor - tal song:
pow'r is burst in twain; E - ter - nal glo - ry to Thy Name:

All hail! all hail! All hail! all hail! Im-man-u-el!
All hail!   all hail!

All Hail, Immanuel

Response

To be sung after each Commandment.   Sir George J. Elvey.

Lord, have mercy, have mercy upon us, And incline our hearts to keep this law. A - MEN.

After last Commandment only.

Gloria Patri

Charles Meineke.

Glo - ry be to the Fa-ther, and to the Son, and to the Ho - ly Ghost; As it

was in the beginning, is now, and ever shall be, world without end, A-men, A-men.

The Lord's Prayer

Gregorian Chant.

1. Our Father which art in Heaven,   hal - lowed be Thy name;
2. Give us this   day our dai - ly bread;
3. And lead us not into temptation, but de - liv - er us from evil;

Thy kingdom come; Thy will be done on   earth as it is in Heaven;
And forgive us our debts, as   we for-give our debtors:
For Thine is the kingdom, and the power, and the glory, for-ev - er, A - - men.

The Treasure of God's Word

The second chapter of the book of Proverbs contains a precious promise for any spiritually awakened soul who is willing to diligently search the Scriptures. The opening five verses of Proverbs 2 state:

> My son, if thou wilt receive my words, and hide my commandments with thee; So that thou incline thine ear unto wisdom, and apply thine heart to understanding; Yea, if thou criest after knowledge, and liftest up thy voice for understanding; If thou seekest her as silver, and searchest for her as for hid treasures; Then shalt thou understand the fear of the LORD, and find the knowledge of God.

Human beings are masters at inventing ways to try to find the true knowledge of God. The Scriptures, however, plainly teach that God has ordained that sinful men must find out the truth concerning their Creator and the way of salvation through a diligent study of the Holy Bible. When spiritually hungry searchers begin to comprehend that the Word of God provides the only truth that can lead to righteousness and peace with God, then they are able to understand how great a treasure they have in God's Word.

For those who have been saved by God's grace, Bible study is more than an intellectual religious exercise. The study of God's Word, with childlike zeal and dependence upon the leading of the Holy Spirit, causes readers to find God's power and wisdom for everyday life. Perhaps Job stated it best when he declared that he valued the Word of God "more than my necessary food" (Job 23:12)—and Job only had a portion of the Old Testament!

The man of God named Job is not the only believer to testify to the value of the Holy Scriptures. Across the ages and at this present hour, the people of God regularly witness to the transforming power of God's Word and Spirit. Christian attorney and nationally known advocate for Christ-centered home education, Michael P. Farris, wrote the following testimony concerning the influence of the Bible upon his fruitful life.

> My earliest memory involving God's Word is from 1957. As a first grader, I attended a Good News Club and was given an assignment to memorize one verse each week. At the end of each

193

ten-week period I was allowed to take a prize from "the treasure chest." I have no memory of any prize from that chest, but the true treasure I gained is still vibrant within my heart. I can still recite verbatim the first Bible verse I ever learned.

Throughout my years in Sunday School and a boy's program called King's Sons, I memorized dozens and dozens of verses and even a few chapters of Scripture. My parents were new believers and strongly encouraged my memorization and made sure that I received thorough instruction in Bible content and doctrine.

I did well academically in school with a good memory as a significant factor. My mother told me—and I believe it—that my early memorization of Scripture was, in her judgment, a key reason that I developed good memory skills. I have no doubt she was right.

As I approached adulthood I began to rely on the Word of God to give me direction for my life. God used both Micah 6:8 and Proverbs 21:15 to confirm His call for me to attend law school. God's Word was my chief source for determining that it was God's will to move from Washington State to the Virginia suburbs of Washington, D.C. And there are many more times God used His Word to illuminate my path.

The things I learned about God's Word and from God's Word are things I am endeavoring to transmit to my children. I want them to:

- read the Word daily,
- memorize the Word,
- understand its meaning, and
- apply it to their lives.

Not only do I want to ensure that my children do these things for themselves, but that they will transmit these values and principles to their children as well. Grandchildren who know, love, and obey God as revealed in His Word will be the real treasure in my life.

May the Lord Jesus Christ give you a hunger to know Him more intimately through a diligent study of His Word. God's Word is indeed a precious treasure, so start digging!

Michael J. McHugh
1999

Scripture Selections

for Responsive Readings

Verses in normal typeface may be read aloud by the worship leader. The verses in bold should be read aloud by the other worshipers.

Selected Psalms

Psalm 1

1 BLESSED is the man that walketh not in the counsel of the ungodly, nor standeth in the way of sinners, nor sitteth in the seat of the scornful.

2 **But his delight is in the law of the LORD; and in his law doth he meditate day and night.**

3 And he shall be like a tree planted by the rivers of water, that bringeth forth his fruit in his season; his leaf also shall not wither; and whatsoever he doeth shall prosper.

4 **The ungodly are not so: but are like the chaff which the wind driveth away.**

5 Therefore the ungodly shall not stand in the judgment, nor sinners in the congregation of the righteous.

6 **For the LORD knoweth the way of the righteous: but the way of the ungodly shall perish.**

Psalm 2

1 WHY do the heathen rage, and the people imagine a vain thing?

2 **The kings of the earth set themselves, and the rulers take counsel together, against the LORD, and against his anointed, saying,**

3 Let us break their bands asunder, and cast away their cords from us.

4 **He that sitteth in the heavens shall laugh: the LORD shall have them in derision.**

5 Then shall he speak unto them in his wrath, and vex them in his sore displeasure.

6 **Yet have I set my king upon my holy hill of Zion.**

7 I will declare the decree: the LORD hath said unto me, Thou art my Son; this day have I begotten thee.

8 **Ask of me, and I shall give thee the heathen for thine inheritance, and the uttermost parts of the earth for thy possession.**

9 Thou shalt break them with a rod of iron; thou shalt dash them in pieces like a potter's vessel.

10 **Be wise now therefore, O ye kings: be instructed, ye judges of the earth.**

11 Serve the LORD with fear, and rejoice with trembling.

12 **Kiss the Son, lest he be angry, and ye perish from the way, when his wrath is kindled but a little. Blessed are all they that put their trust in him.**

Psalm 8

To the chief Musician upon Gittith,
A Psalm of David.

1 O LORD our Lord, how excellent is thy name in all the earth! who hast set thy glory above the heavens.

2 **Out of the mouth of babes and sucklings hast thou ordained strength because of thine enemies, that thou mightest still the enemy and the avenger.**

195

3 When I consider thy heavens, the work of thy fingers, the moon and the stars, which thou hast ordained;

4 **What is man, that thou art mindful of him? and the son of man, that thou visitest him?**

5 For thou hast made him a little lower than the angels, and hast crowned him with glory and honour.

6 **Thou madest him to have dominion over the works of thy hands; thou hast put all things under his feet:**

7 All sheep and oxen, yea, and the beasts of the field;

8 **The fowl of the air, and the fish of the sea, and whatsoever passeth through the paths of the seas.**

9 O LORD our Lord, how excellent is thy name in all the earth!

Psalm 15
A Psalm of David.

1 LORD, who shall abide in thy tabernacle? who shall dwell in thy holy hill?

2 **He that walketh uprightly, and worketh righteousness, and speaketh the truth in his heart.**

3 He that backbiteth not with his tongue, nor doeth evil to his neighbour, nor taketh up a reproach against his neighbour.

4 **In whose eyes a vile person is contemned; but he honoureth them that fear the LORD. He that sweareth to his own hurt, and changeth not.**

5 He that putteth not out his money to usury, nor taketh reward against the innocent. He that doeth these things shall never be moved.

Psalm 19
*To the chief Musician,
A Psalm of David.*

1 THE heavens declare the glory of God; and the firmament sheweth his handiwork.

2 **Day unto day uttereth speech, and night unto night sheweth knowledge.**

3 There is no speech nor language, where their voice is not heard.

4 **Their line is gone out through all the earth, and their words to the end of the world. In them hath he set a tabernacle for the sun,**

5 Which is as a bridegroom coming out of his chamber, and rejoiceth as a strong man to run a race.

6 **His going forth is from the end of the heaven, and his circuit unto the ends of it: and there is nothing hid from the heat thereof.**

7 The law of the LORD is perfect, converting the soul: the testimony of the LORD is sure, making wise the simple.

8 **The statutes of the LORD are right, rejoicing the heart: the commandment of the LORD is pure, enlightening the eyes.**

9 The fear of the LORD is clean, enduring for ever: the judgments of the LORD are true and righteous altogether.

10 **More to be desired are they than gold, yea, than much fine gold: sweeter also than honey and the honeycomb.**

11 Moreover by them is thy servant warned: and in keeping of them there is great reward.

12 **Who can understand his errors? cleanse thou me from secret faults.**

13 Keep back thy servant also from presumptuous sins; let them not have dominion over me: then shall I be upright, and I shall be innocent from the great transgression.

14 **Let the words of my mouth, and the meditation of my heart, be acceptable in thy sight, O LORD, my strength, and my redeemer.**

Psalm 23

A Psalm of David.

1 THE LORD is my shepherd; I shall not want.

2 **He maketh me to lie down in green pastures: he leadeth me beside the still waters.**

3 He restoreth my soul: he leadeth me in the paths of righteousness for his name's sake.

4 **Yea, though I walk through the valley of the shadow of death, I will fear no evil: for thou art with me; thy rod and thy staff they comfort me.**

5 Thou preparest a table before me in the presence of mine enemies: thou anointest my head with oil; my cup runneth over.

6 **Surely goodness and mercy shall follow me all the days of my life: and I will dwell in the house of the LORD for ever.**

Psalm 24

A Psalm of David.

1 THE earth is the LORD'S, and the fulness thereof; the world, and they that dwell therein.

2 **For he hath founded it upon the seas, and established it upon the floods.**

3 Who shall ascend into the hill of the LORD? or who shall stand in his holy place?

4 **He that hath clean hands, and a pure heart; who hath not lifted up his soul unto vanity, nor sworn deceitfully.**

5 He shall receive the blessing from the LORD, and righteousness from the God of his salvation.

6 **This is the generation of them that seek him, that seek thy face, O Jacob. Selah.**

7 Lift up your heads, O ye gates; and be ye lift up, ye everlasting doors; and the King of glory shall come in.

8 **Who is this King of glory? The LORD strong and mighty, the LORD mighty in battle.**

9 Lift up your heads, O ye gates; even lift them up, ye everlasting doors; and the King of glory shall come in.

10 **Who is this King of glory? The LORD of hosts, he is the King of glory. Selah.**

Psalm 34

A Psalm of David, when he changed his behaviour before Abimelech; who drove him away, and he departed.

1 I WILL bless the LORD at all times: his praise shall continually be in my mouth.

2 **My soul shall make her boast in the LORD: the humble shall hear thereof, and be glad.**

3 O magnify the LORD with me, and let us exalt his name together.

4 **I sought the LORD, and he heard me, and delivered me from all my fears.**

5 They looked unto him, and were lightened: and their faces were not ashamed.

6   This poor man cried, and the LORD heard him, and saved him out of all his troubles.

7   The angel of the LORD encampeth round about them that fear him, and delivereth them.

8   O taste and see that the LORD is good: blessed is the man that trusteth in him.

9   O fear the LORD, ye his saints: for there is no want to them that fear him.

10 The young lions do lack, and suffer hunger: but they that seek the LORD shall not want any good thing.

11 Come, ye children, hearken unto me: I will teach you the fear of the LORD.

12 What man is he that desireth life, and loveth many days, that he may see good?

13 Keep thy tongue from evil, and thy lips from speaking guile.

14 Depart from evil, and do good; seek peace, and pursue it.

15 The eyes of the LORD are upon the righteous, and his ears are open unto their cry.

16 The face of the LORD is against them that do evil, to cut off the remembrance of them from the earth.

17 The righteous cry, and the LORD heareth, and delivereth them out of all their troubles.

18 The LORD is nigh unto them that are of a broken heart; and saveth such as be of a contrite spirit.

19 Many are the afflictions of the righteous: but the LORD delivereth him out of them all.

20 He keepeth all his bones: not one of them is broken.

21 Evil shall slay the wicked: and they that hate the righteous shall be desolate.

22 The LORD redeemeth the soul of his servants: and none of them that trust in him shall be desolate.

Psalm 37:1-9
A Psalm of David.

1   FRET not thyself because of evildoers, neither be thou envious against the workers of iniquity.

2   For they shall soon be cut down like the grass, and wither as the green herb.

3   Trust in the LORD, and do good; so shalt thou dwell in the land, and verily thou shalt be fed.

4   Delight thyself also in the LORD; and he shall give thee the desires of thine heart.

5   Commit thy way unto the LORD; trust also in him; and he shall bring it to pass.

6   And he shall bring forth thy righteousness as the light, and thy judgment as the noonday.

7   Rest in the LORD, and wait patiently for him: fret not thyself because of him who prospereth in his way, because of the man who bringeth wicked devices to pass.

8   Cease from anger, and forsake wrath: fret not thyself in any wise to do evil.

9   For evildoers shall be cut off: but those that wait upon the LORD, they shall inherit the earth.

Psalm 39

To the chief Musician, even to Jeduthun,
A Psalm of David.

1 I SAID, I will take heed to my ways, that I sin not with my tongue: I will keep my mouth with a bridle, while the wicked is before me.

2 **I was dumb with silence, I held my peace, even from good; and my sorrow was stirred.**

3 My heart was hot within me, while I was musing the fire burned: then spake I with my tongue.

4 **LORD, make me to know mine end, and the measure of my days, what it is; that I may know how frail I am.**

5 Behold, thou hast made my days as an handbreadth; and mine age is as nothing before thee: verily every man at his best state is altogether vanity. Selah.

6 **Surely every man walketh in a vain shew: surely they are disquieted in vain: he heapeth up riches, and knoweth not who shall gather them.**

7 And now, Lord, what wait I for? my hope is in thee.

8 Deliver me from all my transgressions: make me not the reproach of the foolish.

9 I was dumb, I opened not my mouth; because thou didst it.

10 **Remove thy stroke away from me: I am consumed by the blow of thine hand.**

11 When thou with rebukes dost correct man for iniquity, thou makest his beauty to consume away like a moth: surely every man is vanity. Selah.

12 Hear my prayer, O LORD, and give ear unto my cry; hold not thy peace at my tears: for I am a stranger with thee, and a sojourner, as all my fathers were.

13 O spare me, that I may recover strength, before I go hence, and be no more.

Psalm 40

To the chief Musician,
A Psalm of David.

1 I WAITED patiently for the LORD; and he inclined unto me, and heard my cry.

2 **He brought me up also out of an horrible pit, out of the miry clay, and set my feet upon a rock, and established my goings.**

3 And he hath put a new song in my mouth, even praise unto our God: many shall see it, and fear, and shall trust in the LORD.

4 **Blessed is that man that maketh the LORD his trust, and respecteth not the proud, nor such as turn aside to lies.**

5 Many, O LORD my God, are thy wonderful works which thou hast done, and thy thoughts which are to us-ward: they cannot be reckoned up in order unto thee: if I would declare and speak of them, they are more than can be numbered.

6 **Sacrifice and offering thou didst not desire; mine ears hast thou opened: burnt offering and sin offering hast thou not required.**

7 Then said I, Lo, I come: in the volume of the book it is written of me,

8 **I delight to do thy will, O my God: yea, thy law is within my heart.**

9 I have preached righteousness in the great congregation: lo, I have not

refrained my lips, O LORD, thou knowest.

10 I have not hid thy righteousness within my heart; I have declared thy faithfulness and thy salvation: I have not concealed thy lovingkindness and thy truth from the great congregation.

11 Withhold not thou thy tender mercies from me, O LORD: let thy lovingkindness and thy truth continually preserve me.

12 For innumerable evils have compassed me about: mine iniquities have taken hold upon me, so that I am not able to look up; they are more than the hairs of mine head: therefore my heart faileth me.

13 Be pleased, O LORD, to deliver me: O LORD, make haste to help me.

14 Let them be ashamed and confounded together that seek after my soul to destroy it; let them be driven backward and put to shame that wish me evil.

15 Let them be desolate for a reward of their shame that say unto me, Aha, aha.

16 Let all those that seek thee rejoice and be glad in thee: let such as love thy salvation say continually, The LORD be magnified.

17 But I am poor and needy; yet the Lord thinketh upon me: thou art my help and my deliverer; make no tarrying, O my God.

Psalm 42

*To the chief Musician, Maschil,
for the sons of Korah.*

1 AS the hart panteth after the water brooks, so panteth my soul after thee, O God.

2 My soul thirsteth for God, for the living God: when shall I come and appear before God?

3 My tears have been my meat day and night, while they continually say unto me, Where is thy God?

4 When I remember these things, I pour out my soul in me: for I had gone with the multitude, I went with them to the house of God, with the voice of joy and praise, with a multitude that kept holyday.

5 Why art thou cast down, O my soul? and why art thou disquieted in me? hope thou in God: for I shall yet praise him for the help of his countenance.

6 O my God, my soul is cast down within me: therefore will I remember thee from the land of Jordan, and of the Hermonites, from the hill Mizar.

7 Deep calleth unto deep at the noise of thy waterspouts: all thy waves and thy billows are gone over me.

8 Yet the LORD will command his lovingkindness in the daytime, and in the night his song shall be with me, and my prayer unto the God of my life.

9 I will say unto God my rock, Why hast thou forgotten me? why go I mourning because of the oppression of the enemy?

10 As with a sword in my bones, mine enemies reproach me; while they say daily unto me, Where is thy God?

11 Why art thou cast down, O my soul? and why art thou disquieted within me? hope thou in God: for I shall yet praise him, who is the health of my countenance, and my God.

Psalm 46

*To the chief Musician for the sons of
Korah, A song upon Alamoth.*

1 GOD is our refuge and strength, a
very present help in trouble.

2 **Therefore will not we fear, though
the earth be removed, and though
the mountains be carried into the
midst of the sea;**

3 Though the waters thereof roar and
be troubled, though the mountains
shake with the swelling thereof.
Selah.

4 **There is a river, the streams
whereof shall make glad the city of
God, the holy place of the taberna-
cles of the most High.**

5 God is in the midst of her; she shall
not be moved: God shall help her,
and that right early.

6 **The heathen raged, the kingdoms
were moved: he uttered his voice,
the earth melted.**

7 The LORD of hosts is with us; the
God of Jacob is our refuge. Selah.

8 **Come, behold the works of the
LORD, what desolations he hath
made in the earth.**

9 He maketh wars to cease unto the
end of the earth; he breaketh the
bow, and cutteth the spear in sun-
der; he burneth the chariot in the
fire.

10 **Be still, and know that I am God: I
will be exalted among the heathen,
I will be exalted in the earth.**

11 The LORD of hosts is with us; the
God of Jacob is our refuge. Selah.

Psalm 48

A Song and Psalm for the sons of Korah.

1 GREAT is the LORD, and greatly to
be praised in the city of our God, in
the mountain of his holiness.

2 **Beautiful for situation, the joy of
the whole earth, is mount Zion, on
the sides of the north, the city of
the great King.**

3 God is known in her palaces for a
refuge.

4 **For, lo, the kings were assembled,
they passed by together.**

5 They saw it, and so they marvelled;
they were troubled, and hasted
away.

6 **Fear took hold upon them there,
and pain, as of a woman in travail.**

7 Thou breakest the ships of Tarshish
with an east wind.

8 **As we have heard, so have we seen
in the city of the LORD of hosts, in
the city of our God: God will
establish it for ever. Selah.**

9 We have thought of thy lovingkindness, O God, in the midst of thy
temple.

10 **According to thy name, O God, so
is thy praise unto the ends of the
earth: thy right hand is full of righ
teousness.**

11 Let mount Zion rejoice, let the
daughters of Judah be glad, because
of thy judgments.

12 **Walk about Zion, and go round
about her: tell the towers thereof.**

13 Mark ye well her bulwarks, consider
her palaces; that ye may tell it to the
generation following.

14 **For this God is our God for ever
and ever: he will be our guide even
unto death.**

Psalm 62

*To the chief Musician, to Jeduthun,
A Psalm of David.*

1 TRULY my soul waiteth upon God: from him cometh my salvation.

2 **He only is my rock and my salvation; he is my defence; I shall not be greatly moved.**

3 How long will ye imagine mischief against a man? ye shall be slain all of you: as a bowing wall shall ye be, and as a tottering fence.

4 **They only consult to cast him down from his excellency: they delight in lies: they bless with their mouth, but they curse inwardly. Selah.**

5 My soul, wait thou only upon God; for my expectation is from him.

6 **He only is my rock and my salvation: he is my defence; I shall not be moved.**

7 In God is my salvation and my glory: the rock of my strength, and my refuge, is in God.

8 **Trust in him at all times; ye people, pour out your heart before him: God is a refuge for us. Selah.**

9 Surely men of low degree are vanity, and men of high degree are a lie: to be laid in the balance, they are altogether lighter than vanity.

10 **Trust not in oppression, and become not vain in robbery: if riches increase, set not your heart upon them.**

11 God hath spoken once; twice have I heard this; that power belongeth unto God.

12 **Also unto thee, O Lord, belongeth mercy: for thou renderest to every man according to his work.**

Psalm 65

*To the chief Musician,
A Psalm and Song of David.*

1 PRAISE waiteth for thee, O God, in Sion: and unto thee shall the vow be performed.

2 **O thou that hearest prayer, unto thee shall all flesh come.**

3 Iniquities prevail against me: as for our transgressions, thou shalt purge them away.

4 **Blessed is the man whom thou choosest, and causest to approach unto thee, that he may dwell in thy courts: we shall be satisfied with the goodness of thy house, even of thy holy temple.**

5 By terrible things in righteousness wilt thou answer us, O God of our salvation; who art the confidence of all the ends of the earth, and of them that are afar off upon the sea:

6 **Which by his strength setteth fast the mountains; being girded with power:**

7 Which stilleth the noise of the seas, the noise of their waves, and the tumult of the people.

8 **They also that dwell in the uttermost parts are afraid at thy tokens: thou makest the outgoings of the morning and evening to rejoice.**

9 Thou visitest the earth, and waterest it: thou greatly enrichest it with the river of God, which is full of water: thou preparest them corn, when thou hast so provided for it.

10 **Thou waterest the ridges thereof abundantly: thou settlest the furrows thereof: thou makest it soft with showers: thou blessest the springing thereof.**

11 Thou crownest the year with thy goodness; and thy paths drop fatness.

12 **They drop upon the pastures of the wilderness: and the little hills rejoice on every side.**

13 The pastures are clothed with flocks; the valleys also are covered over with corn; they shout for joy, they also sing.

Psalm 67

To the chief Musician on Neginoth, A Psalm or Song.

1 GOD be merciful unto us, and bless us; and cause his face to shine upon us; Selah.

2 **That thy way may be known upon earth, thy saving health among all nations.**

3 Let the people praise thee, O God; let all the people praise thee.

4 **O let the nations be glad and sing for joy: for thou shalt judge the people righteously, and govern the nations upon earth. Selah.**

5 Let the people praise thee, O God; let all the people praise thee.

6 **Then shall the earth yield her increase; and God, even our own God, shall bless us.**

7 God shall bless us; and all the ends of the earth shall fear him.

Psalm 96

1 O SING unto the LORD a new song: sing unto the LORD, all the earth.

2 **Sing unto the LORD, bless his name; shew forth his salvation from day to day.**

3 Declare his glory among the heathen, his wonders among all people.

4 **For the LORD is great, and greatly to be praised: he is to be feared above all gods.**

5 For all the gods of the nations are idols: but the LORD made the heavens.

6 **Honour and majesty are before him: strength and beauty are in his sanctuary.**

7 Give unto the LORD, O ye kindreds of the people, give unto the LORD glory and strength.

8 **Give unto the LORD the glory due unto his name: bring an offering, and come into his courts.**

9 O worship the LORD in the beauty of holiness: fear before him, all the earth.

10 **Say among the heathen that the LORD reigneth: the world also shall be established that it shall not be moved: he shall judge the people righteously.**

11 Let the heavens rejoice, and let the earth be glad; let the sea roar, and the fulness thereof.

12 **Let the field be joyful, and all that is therein: then shall all the trees of the wood rejoice**

13 Before the LORD: for he cometh, for he cometh to judge the earth: he shall judge the world with righteousness, and the people with his truth.

Psalm 97

1 THE LORD reigneth; let the earth rejoice; let the multitude of isles be glad thereof.

2 **Clouds and darkness are round about him: righteousness and judgment are the habitation of his throne.**

3   A fire goeth before him, and burneth up his enemies round about.

4   **His lightnings enlightened the world: the earth saw, and trembled.**

5   The hills melted like wax at the presence of the LORD, at the presence of the Lord of the whole earth.

6   **The heavens declare his righteousness, and all the people see his glory.**

7   Confounded be all they that serve graven images, that boast themselves of idols: worship him, all ye gods.

8   **Zion heard, and was glad; and the daughters of Judah rejoiced because of thy judgments, O LORD.**

9   For thou, LORD, art high above all the earth: thou art exalted far above all gods.

10 **Ye that love the LORD, hate evil: he preserveth the souls of his saints; he delivereth them out of the hand of the wicked.**

11 Light is sown for the righteous, and gladness for the upright in heart.

12 **Rejoice in the LORD, ye righteous; and give thanks at the remembrance of his holiness.**

Psalm 100
A Psalm of praise.

1   MAKE a joyful noise unto the LORD, all ye lands.

2   **Serve the LORD with gladness: come before his presence with singing.**

3   Know ye that the LORD he is God: it is he that hath made us, and not we ourselves; we are his people, and the sheep of his pasture.

4   **Enter into his gates with thanksgiving, and into his courts with**

praise: **be thankful unto him, and bless his name.**

5   For the LORD is good; his mercy is everlasting; and his truth endureth to all generations.

Psalm 103
A Psalm of David.

1   BLESS the LORD, O my soul: and all that is within me, bless his holy name.

2   **Bless the LORD, O my soul, and forget not all his benefits:**

3   Who forgiveth all thine iniquities; who healeth all thy diseases;

4   **Who redeemeth thy life from destruction; who crowneth thee with lovingkindness and tender mercies;**

5   Who satisfieth thy mouth with good things; so that thy youth is renewed like the eagle's.

6   **The LORD executeth righteousness and judgment for all that are oppressed.**

7   He made known his ways unto Moses, his acts unto the children of Israel.

8   **The LORD is merciful and gracious, slow to anger, and plenteous in mercy.**

9   He will not always chide: neither will he keep his anger for ever.

10 **He hath not dealt with us after our sins; nor rewarded us according to our iniquities.**

11 For as the heaven is high above the earth, so great is his mercy toward them that fear him.

12 **As far as the east is from the west, so far hath he removed our transgressions from us.**

13 Like as a father pitieth his children, so the LORD pitieth them that fear him.

14 **For he knoweth our frame; he remembereth that we are dust.**

15 As for man, his days are as grass: as a flower of the field, so he flourisheth.

16 **For the wind passeth over it, and it is gone; and the place thereof shall know it no more.**

17 But the mercy of the LORD is from everlasting to everlasting upon them that fear him, and his righteousness unto children's children;

18 **To such as keep his covenant, and to those that remember his commandments to do them.**

19 The LORD hath prepared his throne in the heavens; and his kingdom ruleth over all.

20 **Bless the LORD, ye his angels, that excel in strength, that do his commandments, hearkening unto the voice of his word.**

21 Bless ye the LORD, all ye hosts; ye ministers of his, that do his pleasure.

22 **Bless the LORD, all his works in all places of his dominion: bless the LORD, O my soul.**

Psalm 111

1 PRAISE ye the LORD. I will praise the LORD with my whole heart, in the assembly of the upright, and in the congregation.

2 **The works of the LORD are great, sought out of all them that have pleasure therein.**

3 His work is honourable and glorious: and his righteousness endureth for ever.

4 **He hath made his wonderful works to be remembered: the**
LORD **is gracious and full of compassion.**

5 He hath given meat unto them that fear him: he will ever be mindful of his covenant.

6 **He hath shewed his people the power of his works, that he may give them the heritage of the heathen.**

7 The works of his hands are verity and judgment; all his commandments are sure.

8 **They stand fast for ever and ever, and are done in truth and uprightness.**

9 He sent redemption unto his people: he hath commanded his covenant for ever: holy and reverend is his name.

10 **The fear of the LORD is the beginning of wisdom: a good understanding have all they that do his commandments: his praise endureth for ever.**

Psalm 119:1-8

ALEPH.

1 BLESSED are the undefiled in the way, who walk in the law of the LORD.

2 **Blessed are they that keep his testimonies, and that seek him with the whole heart.**

3 They also do no iniquity: they walk in his ways.

4 **Thou hast commanded us to keep thy precepts diligently.**

5 O that my ways were directed to keep thy statutes!

6 **Then shall I not be ashamed, when I have respect unto all thy commandments.**

7   I will praise thee with uprightness of heart, when I shall have learned thy righteous judgments.

8   **I will keep thy statutes: O forsake me not utterly.**

Psalm 121
A Song of degrees.

1   I WILL lift up mine eyes unto the hills, from whence cometh my help.

2   **My help cometh from the LORD, which made heaven and earth.**

3   He will not suffer thy foot to be moved: he that keepeth thee will not slumber.

4   **Behold, he that keepeth Israel shall neither slumber nor sleep.**

5   The LORD is thy keeper: the LORD is thy shade upon thy right hand.

6   **The sun shall not smite thee by day, nor the moon by night.**

7   The LORD shall preserve thee from all evil: he shall preserve thy soul.

8   **The LORD shall preserve thy going out and thy coming in from this time forth, and even for evermore.**

Psalm 122
A Song of degrees of David.

1   I WAS glad when they said unto me, Let us go into the house of the LORD.

2   **Our feet shall stand within thy gates, O Jerusalem.**

3   Jerusalem is builded as a city that is compact together:

4   **Whither the tribes go up, the tribes of the LORD, unto the testimony of Israel, to give thanks unto the name of the LORD.**

5   For there are set thrones of judgment, the thrones of the house of David.

6   **Pray for the peace of Jerusalem: they shall prosper that love thee.**

7   Peace be within thy walls, and prosperity within thy palaces.

8   **For my brethren and companions' sakes, I will now say, Peace be within thee.**

9   Because of the house of the LORD our God I will seek thy good.

Psalm 149

1   PRAISE ye the LORD. Sing unto the LORD a new song, and his praise in the congregation of saints.

2   **Let Israel rejoice in him that made him: let the children of Zion be joyful in their King.**

3   Let them praise his name in the dance: let them sing praises unto him with the timbrel and harp.

4   **For the LORD taketh pleasure in his people: he will beautify the meek with salvation.**

5   Let the saints be joyful in glory: let them sing aloud upon their beds.

6   **Let the high praises of God be in their mouth, and a two-edged sword in their hand;**

7   To execute vengeance upon the heathen, and punishments upon the people;

8   **To bind their kings with chains, and their nobles with fetters of iron;**

9   To execute upon them the judgment written: this honour have all his saints. Praise ye the LORD.

Other Scripture Readings

1 Chronicles 29:10-13

10 Wherefore David blessed the LORD before all the congregation: and David said, Blessed be thou, LORD God of Israel our father, for ever and ever.

11 Thine, O LORD, is the greatness, and the power, and the glory, and the victory, and the majesty: for all that is in the heaven and in the earth is thine; thine is the kingdom, O LORD, and thou art exalted as head above all.

12 Both riches and honour come of thee, and thou reignest over all; and in thine hand is power and might; and in thine hand it is to make great, and to give strength unto all.

13 Now therefore, our God, we thank thee, and praise thy glorious name.

Isaiah 40:1-10

1 COMFORT ye, comfort ye my people, saith your God.

2 Speak ye comfortably to Jerusalem, and cry unto her, that her warfare is accomplished, that her iniquity is pardoned: for she hath received of the LORD'S hand double for all her sins.

3 The voice of him that crieth in the wilderness, Prepare ye the way of the LORD, make straight in the desert a highway for our God.

4 Every valley shall be exalted, and every mountain and hill shall be made low: and the crooked shall be made straight, and the rough places plain:

5 And the glory of the LORD shall be revealed, and all flesh shall see it together: for the mouth of the LORD hath spoken it.

6 The voice said, Cry. And he said, What shall I cry? All flesh is grass, and all the goodliness thereof is as the flower of the field:

7 The grass withereth, the flower fadeth: because the spirit of the LORD bloweth upon it: surely the people is grass.

8 The grass withereth, the flower fadeth: but the word of our God shall stand for ever.

9 O Zion, that bringest good tidings, get thee up into the high mountain; O Jerusalem, that bringest good tidings, lift up thy voice with strength; lift it up, be not afraid; say unto the cities of Judah, Behold your God!

10 Behold, the Lord GOD will come with strong hand, and his arm shall rule for him: behold, his reward is with him, and his work before him.

Isaiah 42:1-10

1 BEHOLD my servant, whom I uphold; mine elect, in whom my soul delighteth; I have put my spirit upon him: he shall bring forth judgment to the Gentiles.

2 He shall not cry, nor lift up, nor cause his voice to be heard in the street.

3 A bruised reed shall he not break, and the smoking flax shall he not quench: he shall bring forth judgment unto truth.

4 He shall not fail nor be discouraged, till he have set judgment in the earth: and the isles shall wait for his law.

5 Thus saith God the LORD, he that created the heavens, and stretched them out; he that spread forth the earth and that which cometh out of it; he that giveth breath unto the

people upon it, and spirit to them that walk therein:

6 I the LORD have called thee in righteousness, and will hold thine hand, and will keep thee, and give thee for a covenant of the people, for a light of the Gentiles;

7 To open the blind eyes, to bring out the prisoners from the prison, and them that sit in darkness out of the prison house.

8 I am the LORD: that is my name: and my glory will I not give to another, neither my praise unto graven images.

9 Behold, the former things are come to pass, and new things do I declare: before they spring forth I tell you of them.

10 Sing unto the LORD a new song, and his praise from the end of the earth, ye that go down to the sea, and all that is therein; the isles, and the inhabitants thereof.

Isaiah 52:7-10

7 How beautiful upon the mountains are the feet of him that bringeth good tidings, that publisheth peace; that bringeth good tidings of good, that publisheth salvation; that saith unto Zion, Thy God reigneth!

8 Thy watchmen shall lift up the voice; with the voice together shall they sing: for they shall see eye to eye, when the LORD shall bring again Zion.

9 Break forth into joy, sing together, ye waste places of Jerusalem: for the LORD hath comforted his people, he hath redeemed Jerusalem.

10 The LORD hath made bare his holy arm in the eyes of all the nations;

and all the ends of the earth shall see the salvation of our God.

Isaiah 53

1 WHO hath believed our report? and to whom is the arm of the LORD revealed?

2 For he shall grow up before him as a tender plant, and as a root out of a dry ground: he hath no form nor comeliness; and when we shall see him, there is no beauty that we should desire him.

3 He is despised and rejected of men; a man of sorrows, and acquainted with grief: and we hid as it were our faces from him; he was despised, and we esteemed him not.

4 Surely he hath borne our griefs, and carried our sorrows: yet we did esteem him stricken, smitten of God, and afflicted.

5 But he was wounded for our transgressions, he was bruised for our iniquities: the chastisement of our peace was upon him; and with his stripes we are healed.

6 All we like sheep have gone astray; we have turned every one to his own way; and the LORD hath laid on him the iniquity of us all.

7 He was oppressed, and he was afflicted, yet he opened not his mouth: he is brought as a lamb to the slaughter, and as a sheep before her shearers is dumb, so he openeth not his mouth.

8 He was taken from prison and from judgment: and who shall declare his generation? for he was cut off out of the land of the living: for the transgression of my people was he stricken.

9 And he made his grave with the wicked, and with the rich in his

death; because he had done no violence, neither was any deceit in his mouth.

10 **Yet it pleased the LORD to bruise him; he hath put him to grief: when thou shalt make his soul an offering for sin, he shall see his seed, he shall prolong his days, and the pleasure of the LORD shall prosper in his hand.**

11 He shall see of the travail of his soul, and shall be satisfied: by his knowledge shall my righteous servant justify many; for he shall bear their iniquities.

12 Therefore will I divide him a portion with the great, and he shall divide the spoil with the strong; because he hath poured out his soul unto death: and he was numbered with the transgressors; and he bare the sin of many, and made intercession for the transgressors.

Isaiah 55:1-11

1 HO, every one that thirsteth, come ye to the waters, and he that hath no money; come ye, buy, and eat; yea, come, buy wine and milk without money and without price.

2 **Wherefore do ye spend money for that which is not bread? and your labour for that which satisfieth not? hearken diligently unto me, and eat ye that which is good, and let your soul delight itself in fatness.**

3 Incline your ear, and come unto me: hear, and your soul shall live; and I will make an everlasting covenant with you, even the sure mercies of David.

4 **Behold, I have given him for a witness to the people, a leader and commander to the people.**

5 Behold, thou shalt call a nation that thou knowest not, and nations that knew not thee shall run unto thee because of the LORD thy God, and for the Holy One of Israel; for he hath glorified thee.

6 **Seek ye the LORD while he may be found, call ye upon him while he is near:**

7 Let the wicked forsake his way, and the unrighteous man his thoughts: and let him return unto the LORD, and he will have mercy upon him; and to our God, for he will abundantly pardon.

8 **For my thoughts are not your thoughts, neither are your ways my ways, saith the LORD.**

9 For as the heavens are higher than the earth, so are my ways higher than your ways, and my thoughts than your thoughts.

10 **For as the rain cometh down, and the snow from heaven, and returneth not thither, but watereth the earth, and maketh it bring forth and bud, that it may give seed to the sower, and bread to the eater:**

11 So shall my word be that goeth forth out of my mouth: it shall not return unto me void, but it shall accomplish that which I please, and it shall prosper in the thing whereto I sent it.

Matthew 5:1-12

1 AND seeing the multitudes, he went up into a mountain: and when he was set, his disciples came unto him:

2 **And he opened his mouth, and taught them, saying,**

3 Blessed are the poor in spirit: for theirs is the kingdom of heaven.

4 **Blessed are they that mourn: for they shall be comforted.**

5 Blessed are the meek: for they shall inherit the earth.

6 **Blessed are they which do hunger and thirst after righteousness: for they shall be filled.**

7 Blessed are the merciful: for they shall obtain mercy.

8 **Blessed are the pure in heart: for they shall see God.**

9 Blessed are the peacemakers: for they shall be called the children of God.

10 **Blessed are they which are persecuted for righteousness' sake: for theirs is the kingdom of heaven.**

11 Blessed are ye, when men shall revile you, and persecute you, and shall say all manner of evil against you falsely, for my sake.

12 **Rejoice, and be exceeding glad: for great is your reward in heaven: for so persecuted they the prophets which were before you.**

Matthew 18:1-6

1 AT the same time came the disciples unto Jesus, saying, Who is the greatest in the kingdom of heaven?

2 **And Jesus called a little child unto him, and set him in the midst of them,**

3 And said, Verily I say unto you, Except ye be converted, and become as little children, ye shall not enter into the kingdom of heaven.

4 **Whosoever therefore shall humble himself as this little child, the same is greatest in the kingdom of heaven.**

5 And whoso shall receive one such little child in my name receiveth me.

6 **But whoso shall offend one of these little ones which believe in me, it were better for him that a millstone were hanged about his neck, and that he were drowned in the depth of the sea.**

Mark 10:13-16

13 And they brought young children to him, that he should touch them: and his disciples rebuked those that brought them.

14 **But when Jesus saw it, he was much displeased, and said unto them, Suffer the little children to come unto me, and forbid them not: for of such is the kingdom of God.**

15 Verily I say unto you, Whosoever shall not receive the kingdom of God as a little child, he shall not enter therein.

16 **And he took them up in his arms, put his hands upon them, and blessed them.**

John 3:14-21

14 And as Moses lifted up the serpent in the wilderness, even so must the Son of man be lifted up:

15 **That whosoever believeth in him should not perish, but have eternal life.**

16 For God so loved the world, that he gave his only begotten Son, that whosoever believeth in him should not perish, but have everlasting life.

17 **For God sent not his Son into the world to condemn the world; but that the world through him might be saved.**

18 He that believeth on him is not condemned: but he that believeth not is condemned already, because

he hath not believed in the name of the only begotten Son of God.

19 **And this is the condemnation, that light is come into the world, and men loved darkness rather than light, because their deeds were evil.**

20 For every one that doeth evil hateth the light, neither cometh to the light, lest his deeds should be reproved.

21 **But he that doeth truth cometh to the light, that his deeds may be made manifest, that they are wrought in God.**

John 10:1-11

1 VERILY, verily, I say unto you, He that entereth not by the door into the sheepfold, but climbeth up some other way, the same is a thief and a robber.

2 **But he that entereth in by the door is the shepherd of the sheep.**

3 To him the porter openeth; and the sheep hear his voice: and he calleth his own sheep by name, and leadeth them out.

4 **And when he putteth forth his own sheep, he goeth before them, and the sheep follow him: for they know his voice.**

5 And a stranger will they not follow, but will flee from him: for they know not the voice of strangers.

6 **This parable spake Jesus unto them: but they understood not what things they were which he spake unto them.**

7 Then said Jesus unto them again, Verily, verily, I say unto you, I am the door of the sheep.

8 **All that ever came before me are thieves and robbers: but the sheep did not hear them.**

9 I am the door: by me if any man enter in, he shall be saved, and shall go in and out, and find pasture.

10 **The thief cometh not, but for to steal, and to kill, and to destroy: I am come that they might have life, and that they might have it more abundantly.**

11 I am the good shepherd: the good shepherd giveth his life for the sheep.

John 15:1-17

1 I AM the true vine, and my Father is the husbandman.

2 **Every branch in me that beareth not fruit he taketh away: and every branch that beareth fruit, he purgeth it, that it may bring forth more fruit.**

3 Now ye are clean through the word which I have spoken unto you.

4 **Abide in me, and I in you. As the branch cannot bear fruit of itself, except it abide in the vine; no more can ye, except ye abide in me.**

5 I am the vine, ye are the branches: He that abideth in me, and I in him, the same bringeth forth much fruit: for without me ye can do nothing.

6 **If a man abide not in me, he is cast forth as a branch, and is withered; and men gather them, and cast them into the fire, and they are burned.**

7 If ye abide in me, and my words abide in you, ye shall ask what ye will, and it shall be done unto you.

8 **Herein is my Father glorified, that ye bear much fruit; so shall ye be my disciples.**

9 As the Father hath loved me, so have I loved you: continue ye in my love.

10 **If ye keep my commandments, ye shall abide in my love; even as I have kept my Father's commandments, and abide in his love.**

11 These things have I spoken unto you, that my joy might remain in you, and that your joy might be full.

12 **This is my commandment, That ye love one another, as I have loved you.**

13 Greater love hath no man than this, that a man lay down his life for his friends.

14 **Ye are my friends, if ye do whatsoever I command you.**

15 Henceforth I call you not servants; for the servant knoweth not what his lord doeth: but I have called you friends; for all things that I have heard of my Father I have made known unto you.

16 **Ye have not chosen me, but I have chosen you, and ordained you, that ye should go and bring forth fruit, and that your fruit should remain: that whatsoever ye shall ask of the Father in my name, he may give it you.**

17 These things I command you, that ye love one another.

Romans 8:1-18

1 THERE is therefore now no condemnation to them which are in Christ Jesus, who walk not after the flesh, but after the Spirit.

2 **For the law of the Spirit of life in Christ Jesus hath made me free from the law of sin and death.**

3 For what the law could not do, in that it was weak through the flesh,

God sending his own Son in the likeness of sinful flesh, and for sin, condemned sin in the flesh:

4 **That the righteousness of the law might be fulfilled in us, who walk not after the flesh, but after the Spirit.**

5 For they that are after the flesh do mind the things of the flesh; but they that are after the Spirit the things of the Spirit.

6 **For to be carnally minded is death; but to be spiritually minded is life and peace.**

7 Because the carnal mind is enmity against God: for it is not subject to the law of God, neither indeed can be.

8 **So then they that are in the flesh cannot please God.**

9 But ye are not in the flesh, but in the Spirit, if so be that the Spirit of God dwell in you. Now if any man have not the Spirit of Christ, he is none of his.

10 **And if Christ be in you, the body is dead because of sin; but the Spirit is life because of righteousness.**

11 But if the Spirit of him that raised up Jesus from the dead dwell in you, he that raised up Christ from the dead shall also quicken your mortal bodies by his Spirit that dwelleth in you.

12 **Therefore, brethren, we are debtors, not to the flesh, to live after the flesh.**

13 For if ye live after the flesh, ye shall die: but if ye through the Spirit do mortify the deeds of the body, ye shall live.

14 **For as many as are led by the Spirit of God, they are the sons of God.**

15 For ye have not received the spirit of bondage again to fear; but ye have received the Spirit of adoption, whereby we cry, Abba, Father.

16 **The Spirit itself beareth witness with our spirit, that we are the children of God:**

17 And if children, then heirs; heirs of God, and joint-heirs with Christ; if so be that we suffer with him, that we may be also glorified together.

18 **For I reckon that the sufferings of this present time are not worthy to be compared with the glory which shall be revealed in us.**

Romans 8:35-39

35 Who shall separate us from the love of Christ? shall tribulation, or distress, or persecution, or famine, or nakedness, or peril, or sword?

36 **As it is written, For thy sake we are killed all the day long; we are accounted as sheep for the slaughter.**

37 Nay, in all these things we are more than conquerors through him that loved us.

38 **For I am persuaded, that neither death, nor life, nor angels, nor principalities, nor powers, nor things present, nor things to come,**

39 Nor height, nor depth, nor any other creature, shall be able to separate us from the love of God, which is in Christ Jesus our Lord.

Romans 10:8-17

8 But what saith it? The word is nigh thee, even in thy mouth, and in thy heart: that is, the word of faith, which we preach;

9 **That if thou shalt confess with thy mouth the Lord Jesus, and shalt believe in thine heart that God hath raised him from the dead, thou shalt be saved.**

10 For with the heart man believeth unto righteousness; and with the mouth confession is made unto salvation.

11 **For the scripture saith, Whosoever believeth on him shall not be ashamed.**

12 For there is no difference between the Jew and the Greek: for the same Lord over all is rich unto all that call upon him.

13 **For whosoever shall call upon the name of the Lord shall be saved.**

14 How then shall they call on him in whom they have not believed? and how shall they believe in him of whom they have not heard? and how shall they hear without a preacher?

15 **And how shall they preach, except they be sent? as it is written, How beautiful are the feet of them that preach the gospel of peace, and bring glad tidings of good things!**

16 But they have not all obeyed the gospel. For Esaias saith, Lord, who hath believed our report?

17 **So then faith cometh by hearing, and hearing by the word of God.**

Romans 12:1-21

1 I BESEECH you therefore, brethren, by the mercies of God, that ye present your bodies a living sacrifice, holy, acceptable unto God, which is your reasonable service.

2 **And be not conformed to this world: but be ye transformed by the renewing of your mind, that ye may prove what is that good, and acceptable, and perfect, will of God.**

3   For I say, through the grace given
     unto me, to every man that is
     among you, not to think of himself
     more highly than he ought to think;
     but to think soberly, according as
     God hath dealt to every man the
     measure of faith.

4   **For as we have many members in
     one body, and all members have
     not the same office:**

5   So we, being many, are one body in
     Christ, and every one members one
     of another.

6   **Having then gifts differing accord-
     ing to the grace that is given to us,
     whether prophecy, let us prophesy
     according to the proportion of
     faith;**

7   Or ministry, let us wait on our min-
     istering: or he that teacheth, on
     teaching;

8   **Or he that exhorteth, on exhorta-
     tion: he that giveth, let him do it
     with simplicity; he that ruleth,
     with diligence; he that sheweth
     mercy, with cheerfulness.**

9   Let love be without dissimulation.
     Abhor that which is evil; cleave to
     that which is good.

10   **Be kindly affectioned one to
     another with brotherly love; in
     honour preferring one another;**

11   Not slothful in business; fervent in
     spirit; serving the Lord;

12   **Rejoicing in hope; patient in tribu-
     lation; continuing instant in
     prayer;**

13   Distributing to the necessity of
     saints; given to hospitality.

14   **Bless them which persecute you:
     bless, and curse not.**

15   Rejoice with them that do rejoice,
     and weep with them that weep.

16   **Be of the same mind one toward
     another. Mind not high things, but
     condescend to men of low estate.
     Be not wise in your own conceits.**

17   Recompense to no man evil for evil.
     Provide things honest in the sight of
     all men.

18   **If it be possible, as much as lieth in
     you, live peaceably with all men.**

19   Dearly beloved, avenge not your-
     selves, but rather give place unto
     wrath: for it is written, Vengeance is
     mine; I will repay, saith the Lord.

20   **Therefore if thine enemy hunger,
     feed him; if he thirst, give him
     drink: for in so doing thou shalt
     heap coals of fire on his head.**

21   Be not overcome of evil, but over-
     come evil with good.

1 Corinthians 13

1   THOUGH I speak with the tongues
     of men and of angels, and have not
     charity, I am become as sounding
     brass, or a tinkling cymbal.

2   **And though I have the gift of
     prophecy, and understand all mys-
     teries, and all knowledge; and
     though I have all faith, so that I
     could remove mountains, and have
     not charity, I am nothing.**

3   And though I bestow all my goods
     to feed the poor, and though I give
     my body to be burned, and have
     not charity, it profiteth me nothing.

4   **Charity suffereth long, and is kind;
     charity envieth not; charity vaunt-
     eth not itself, is not puffed up,**

5   Doth not behave itself unseemly,
     seeketh not her own, is not easily
     provoked, thinketh no evil;

6   **Rejoiceth not in iniquity, but
     rejoiceth in the truth;**

7 Beareth all things, believeth all things, hopeth all things, endureth all things.

8 **Charity never faileth: but whether there be prophecies, they shall fail; whether there be tongues, they shall cease; whether there be knowledge, it shall vanish away.**

9 For we know in part, and we prophesy in part.

10 **But when that which is perfect is come, then that which is in part shall be done away.**

11 When I was a child, I spake as a child, I understood as a child, I thought as a child: but when I became a man, I put away childish things.

12 **For now we see through a glass, darkly; but then face to face: now I know in part; but then shall I know even as also I am known.**

13 And now abideth faith, hope, charity, these three; but the greatest of these is charity.

Galatians 6:1-10

1 BRETHREN, if a man be overtaken in a fault, ye which are spiritual, restore such an one in the spirit of meekness, considering thyself, lest thou also be tempted.

2 **Bear ye one another's burdens, and so fulfill the law of Christ.**

3 For if a man think himself to be something, when he is nothing, he deceiveth himself.

4 **But let every man prove his own work, and then shall he have rejoicing in himself alone, and not in another.**

5 For every man shall bear his own burden.

6 **Let him that is taught in the word communicate unto him that teacheth in all good things.**

7 Be not deceived; God is not mocked: for whatsoever a man soweth, that shall he also reap.

8 **For he that soweth to his flesh shall of the flesh reap corruption; but he that soweth to the Spirit shall of the Spirit reap life everlasting.**

9 And let us not be weary in well doing: for in due season we shall reap, if we faint not.

10 **As we have therefore opportunity, let us do good unto all men, especially unto them who are of the household of faith.**

Ephesians 6:10-18

10 Finally, my brethren, be strong in the Lord, and in the power of his might.

11 **Put on the whole armour of God, that ye may be able to stand against the wiles of the devil.**

12 For we wrestle not against flesh and blood, but against principalities, against powers, against the rulers of the darkness of this world, against spiritual wickedness in high places.

13 **Wherefore take unto you the whole armour of God, that ye may be able to withstand in the evil day, and having done all, to stand.**

14 Stand therefore, having your loins girt about with truth, and having on the breastplate of righteousness;

15 **And your feet shod with the preparation of the gospel of peace;**

16 Above all, taking the shield of faith, wherewith ye shall be able to quench all the fiery darts of the wicked.

17 **And take the helmet of salvation, and the sword of the Spirit, which is the word of God:**

18 Praying always with all prayer and supplication in the Spirit, and watching thereunto with all perseverance and supplication for all saints.

Philippians 2:5-16

5 Let this mind be in you, which was also in Christ Jesus:

6 **Who, being in the form of God, thought it not robbery to be equal with God:**

7 But made himself of no reputation, and took upon him the form of a servant, and was made in the likeness of men:

8 **And being found in fashion as a man, he humbled himself, and became obedient unto death, even the death of the cross.**

9 Wherefore God also hath highly exalted him, and given him a name which is above every name:

10 **That at the name of Jesus every knee should bow, of things in heaven, and things in earth, and things under the earth;**

11 And that every tongue should confess that Jesus Christ is Lord, to the glory of God the Father.

12 **Wherefore, my beloved, as ye have always obeyed, not as in my presence only, but now much more in my absence, work out your own salvation with fear and trembling.**

13 For it is God which worketh in you both to will and to do of his good pleasure.

14 **Do all things without murmurings and disputings:**

15 That ye may be blameless and harmless, the sons of God, without rebuke, in the midst of a crooked and perverse nation, among whom ye shine as lights in the world;

16 **Holding forth the word of life; that I may rejoice in the day of Christ, that I have not run in vain, neither laboured in vain.**

Philippians 4:4-13

4 Rejoice in the Lord alway: and again I say, Rejoice.

5 **Let your moderation be known unto all men. The Lord is at hand.**

6 Be careful for nothing; but in every thing by prayer and supplication with thanksgiving let your requests be made known unto God.

7 **And the peace of God, which passeth all understanding, shall keep your hearts and minds through Christ Jesus.**

8 Finally, brethren, whatsoever things are true, whatsoever things are honest, whatsoever things are just, whatsoever things are pure, whatsoever things are lovely, whatsoever things are of good report; if there be any virtue, and if there be any praise, think on these things.

9 **Those things, which ye have both learned, and received, and heard, and seen in me, do: and the God of peace shall be with you.**

10 But I rejoiced in the Lord greatly, that now at the last your care of me hath flourished again; wherein ye were also careful, but ye lacked opportunity.

11 **Not that I speak in respect of want: for I have learned, in whatsoever state I am, therewith to be content.**

12 I know both how to be abased, and I know how to abound: every where

and in all things I am instructed both to be full and to be hungry, both to abound and to suffer need.

13 **I can do all things through Christ which strengtheneth me.**

1 Thessalonians 5:8-21

8 But let us, who are of the day, be sober, putting on the breastplate of faith and love; and for an helmet, the hope of salvation.

9 **For God hath not appointed us to wrath, but to obtain salvation by our Lord Jesus Christ,**

10 Who died for us, that, whether we wake or sleep, we should live together with him.

11 **Wherefore comfort yourselves together, and edify one another, even as also ye do.**

12 And we beseech you, brethren, to know them which labour among you, and are over you in the Lord, and admonish you;

13 **And to esteem them very highly in love for their work's sake. And be at peace among yourselves.**

14 Now we exhort you, brethren, warn them that are unruly, comfort the feebleminded, support the weak, be patient toward all men.

15 **See that none render evil for evil unto any man; but ever follow that which is good, both among yourselves, and to all men.**

16 Rejoice evermore.

17 **Pray without ceasing.**

18 In everything give thanks: for this is the will of God in Christ Jesus concerning you.

19 **Quench not the Spirit.**

20 Despise not prophesyings.

21 **Prove all things; hold fast that which is good.**

1 John 1

1 THAT which was from the beginning, which we have heard, which we have seen with our eyes, which we have looked upon, and our hands have handled, of the Word of life;

2 **(For the life was manifested, and we have seen it, and bear witness, and shew unto you that eternal life, which was with the Father, and was manifested unto us;)**

3 That which we have seen and heard declare we unto you, that ye also may have fellowship with us: and truly our fellowship is with the Father, and with his Son Jesus Christ.

4 **And these things write we unto you, that your joy may be full.**

5 This then is the message which we have heard of him, and declare unto you, that God is light, and in him is no darkness at all.

6 **If we say that we have fellowship with him, and walk in darkness, we lie, and do not the truth:**

7 But if we walk in the light, as he is in the light, we have fellowship one with another, and the blood of Jesus Christ his Son cleanseth us from all sin.

8 **If we say that we have no sin, we deceive ourselves, and the truth is not in us.**

9 If we confess our sins, he is faithful and just to forgive us our sins, and to cleanse us from all unrighteousness.

10 **If we say that we have not sinned, we make him a liar, and his word is not in us.**

1 John 5:1-15

1 WHOSOEVER believeth that Jesus is the Christ is born of God: and every one that loveth him that begat loveth him also that is begotten of him.

2 **By this we know that we love the children of God, when we love God, and keep his commandments.**

3 For this is the love of God, that we keep his commandments: and his commandments are not grievous.

4 **For whatsoever is born of God overcometh the world: and this is the victory that overcometh the world, even our faith.**

5 Who is he that overcometh the world, but he that believeth that Jesus is the Son of God?

6 **This is he that came by water and blood, even Jesus Christ; not by water only, but by water and blood. And it is the Spirit that beareth witness, because the Spirit is truth.**

7 For there are three that bear record in heaven, the Father, the Word, and the Holy Ghost: and these three are one.

8 **And there are three that bear witness in earth, the spirit, and the** water, and the blood: and these three agree in one.

9 If we receive the witness of men, the witness of God is greater: for this is the witness of God which he hath testified of his Son.

10 **He that believeth on the Son of God hath the witness in himself: he that believeth not God hath made him a liar; because he believeth not the record that God gave of his Son.**

11 And this is the record, that God hath given to us eternal life, and this life is in his Son.

12 **He that hath the Son hath life; and he that hath not the Son of God hath not life.**

13 These things have I written unto you that believe on the name of the Son of God; that ye may know that ye have eternal life, and that ye may believe on the name of the Son of God.

14 **And this is the confidence that we have in him, that, if we ask any thing according to his will, he heareth us:**

15 And if we know that he hear us, whatsoever we ask, we know that we have the petitions that we desired of him.

A Prayer of
Repentance and Faith

Without salvation, all human beings are spiritually lost. Without Christ, all will die in their sins and enter into a hellish eternity. Jesus calls lost sinners to "come," and to find rest and forgiveness in Him.

As taught in the Scriptures, **true repentance and saving faith are the results of God's sovereign work of grace in the heart**. That work is a creative act of God, even as in His original work of creation. God generates new life, and the gift of repentance and faith are implanted in the heart. It is totally a work of God. Man cannot earn salvation; God's work of salvation is His gift to man. Such **regeneration** (or being "born again") is a secret and inscrutable work of God that is never directly perceived by man (like the mysterious movement of the wind—John 3:8); it can only be perceived in its effects—true repentance and saving faith.

Repentance and faith, also known as **conversion**, are not the causes of salvation. The root or cause is God's amazing grace. Conversion is simply the visible result of that gracious and marvelous work.

Are you a Christian? Have you been saved by God's grace? If so, true repentance and saving faith will be the results. You will **forsake** the old sinful life, **believe** God's truth (the Bible), and **receive** it as you **turn** to a life devoted to God.

Below you will find a suggested prayer of repentance and faith.

Dear Heavenly Father,

I believe that you are the one true God, and that you sent your One and only Son to suffer in the place of all sinners who trust in Him as their Savior. I believe that Jesus endured what I ought to have endured, and made atonement to God for my sinful nature and all the sins that I would ever commit. I believe that Christ died, and that He rose bodily from the dead on the third day.

Lord, I know that I have no merit of my own. I deserve to die. Because of my sinful nature, I deserve to perish. I deserve to be destroyed. But you forgive sinners for your own name's sake.

You cannot find anything in us that is spiritually good, or anything that can move you to pity. But, oh, by your grace, have mercy upon me and forgive me. Wash me and make me clean.

Lord, you have said that "him that cometh to me, I will in no wise cast out." And also, "Let the wicked forsake his ways, and the unrighteous man his thoughts." I cast aside all my former confidences, and all my boastings and pride, and come to you as a sinner. I come to you, Lord God, as an utterly lost, undone, spiritually bankrupt sinner; and I look to the atoning sacrifice of Jesus for my salvation.

I thank you, heavenly Father, for this salvation that you have extended to me through Jesus Christ. I thank you that by your grace I have been given life. As one dead in my sins, you have sovereignly saved me. I have not chosen you, but you have chosen me. I love you because you first loved me. And I praise you for your gifts of repentance and faith.

In Jesus name, Amen!

Please remember, **it is not your prayer to God that will save you**. "Salvation is of the Lord," as the Bible teaches, and as already noted. However, if God has saved you by His grace (regeneration), and has created in you the gifts of repentance and faith (conversion), this prayer will express the desire of your heart. And, even as the disciples said, "Lord, teach us to pray," we are offering this prayer simply to help you as you seek to communicate with God and verbally begin to express the gifts of repentance and faith that He has sovereignly granted.

Index

Scripture Selections

Selected Psalms

Other Scripture Readings

Music from *Christian Liberty Press*

Still Waters, by pianist Mike Sherman

This audio CD contains seventeen piano numbers that focus upon the great hymns of the faith. Classic selections include hymns such as "How Great Thou Art," "Sweet Hour of Prayer," and "Jesus, Keep Me Near the Cross." (Christian Liberty Press)

From Glory to Glory: The Gospel through Music, by Steve Turley

This audio CD tells the story of God's dealings with man, from creation, through mankind's fall, and ultimately to the promise of redemption through His Son Jesus Christ. (Fretboard Fellowship) See our catalog or visit our Web site for other CDs and guitar workbooks produced by Steve Turley.

Judy Rogers

Children, teens, and parents have enjoyed learning Biblical truths through Judy Rogers's songs since 1968, when her first album *Why Can't I See God?* was released. Her music covers the major teachings of the Bible. See our catalog or visit our Web site for a complete list of her CDs.

For more music from *Christian Liberty Press*

Contact us by mail at:

Christian Liberty Press
502 West Euclid Avenue
Arlington Heights, IL 60004

Or, you may call us at:

(847) 259-4444, press 6.

Our fax order line is (847) 259-2941.

You may also order on-line at:

www.christianlibertypress.com

For a FREE catalog, call (800) 832-2741.